IF YOU ARE ME, THEN WHO AM I

The Personal and Business
Reality of Identity Theft

JOHN P. GARDNER JR.
JAMES D. MCCARTNEY
JEFFREY M. OMTVEDT

iUniverse, Inc.
New York   Bloomington

iUniverse books may be ordered through booksellers or by contacting:

iUniverse
1663 Liberty Drive
Bloomington, IN 47403
www.iuniverse.com
1-800-Authors (1-800-288-4677)

ISBN: 978-1-4401-1773-2 (pbk)
ISBN: 978-1-4401-1774-9 (ebk)

Printed in the United States of America

iUniverse rev. date: 2/17/2009

Acknowledgements

John Gardner

Every new direction in life begins with an idea, an opportunity to explore a thought or direction not contemplated previously. This one was made possible first by Harland Stonecipher, who afforded me the opportunity to travel the nation gathering knowledge about and information on identity theft and the related issues surrounding it. Without that opportunity, I would have never "connected the dots" between identity theft and "The DataBased You." My "research" began with F Lee Bailey, the famed trial attorney, as we travelled to a dozen cities across North America. Lee, thanks for the time and the stories. The research continued with me travelling to 32 states in one year collecting stories, information and from one person to the next, the knowledge that identity theft was personal, never ending and growing at an ever increasing rate. Where do you begin in thanking the innumerable people who shared their Identity Theft nightmares, those who brought information to me from every corner of North America? If you are one of the soldiers in the army of people who shared your thoughts, experiences or information with me on this subject, Thank You, you helped us recognize each of the areas we have chosen to expound on.

Jillian Manus and her team, thanks for giving us a "dose of reality." You have impacted us all.

My wife Elizabeth, supported not only my passion, but also was a constant sounding board keeping me grounded on what mattered. Jeffrey Omtvedt, my co-author, is responsible for the idea of the book and my belief that with his help we could educate others on what then was being portrayed as a victimless crime, limited to financial in damage. We knew that was not true but few others did. Our walks on Cherry Grove Beach will never be forgotten.

Rock Jolly organized literally thousands of pieces of information into usable material with which we began the process of connecting the dots for people across North America. He made me believe and exhibited a "servant's heart," in the best sense, like none other I have ever met.

Coral Rice, you are an example that I wish I could emulate in a better way. To Steve Houston, thank you for the gift of your time and your spirit. Todd Parrish, my sincere thanks for all of your creative efforts. Frank and Theresa AuCoin, my best friends, thank you for supporting me in every crazy idea I have had.

Jim McCartney brought an expertise, a viewpoint, and a work ethic that simply made the book what it is. Jim, like me in its variety, but at a much higher level, has a set of experiences different than most. He graduated from the Air Force Academy, became a Naval Surface Warfare Officer, then ran the nuclear reactor on the USS Nimitz (Aircraft Carrier) and left to work in Washington, DC for BearingPoint, a government consulting company. Truth be known, he is a driving force behind some significant pieces of the Federal Government's Privacy Policies being written today. He gives me hope that there are people who hold a balanced view of government necessity, corporate desire, and individual privacy. Identity thieves could give governmental authorities and the profit side of corporate America the excuse they might use to trample individual privacy. Jim understands that if knowledge is power and absolute power absolutely corrupts then absolute knowledge will absolutely corrupt. There must be a balance between stopping identity thieves and collecting more information than is necessary or good for anyone, individually, corporately, and even on a governmental level. He is, in my opinion, the most knowledgeable person globally on the issues of identity theft, privacy, and data protection and how they all interact with each other.

My children have born the brunt of my focus on this problem, called identity theft, in more ways than I care to admit. I simply say thank you for your sacrifices, even if not of your choice. I love you all. What gifts from God!

Last, my father is looking down from Heaven chuckling. He is responsible for my total dependence on God. He was a civil rights attorney, representing the NAACP in the 60's and early 70's. I remember going to the city and county jails on Saturday nights, when abusing blacks was all but a sport. I remember a Coroner Jury Trial, on Christmas day. He would take the cases no one else would because it was the right thing to do. I remember him defending a college student framed for drug distribution. He was threatened with his life by the "hanging judge," if he didn't plea the case out. I was there. The judge was popular in his county for "cleaning up the drug problem" and with the judiciary. Daddy filed a civil rights action in Federal Court to have him removed, along with all the Newspaper Articles I worked tirelessly to gather, telling of the Judge's talks to Rotary and other civic organizations of his efforts to stamp out drugs. The judge backed down, the charges were "miraculously" dropped and I learned no matter the consequences, make the system work. Protect those who have no voice. When he went on the bench as an appellate judge he continued to do what he believed was the right thing. He taught me to listen and consider all view points because there is some validity in most of them. Because of that you have many viewpoints represented in this book.

The Co-Authors are an unlikely bunch to put a book together. We are different, representing different generations, different political views, and different professional backgrounds. We have had competing views we wish to share with you and I thank them for working through what at times have been rough points because we all feel passionately that you need to know the truth, "as we perceive it". Enjoy!

James McCartney

Above all else I must thank God for the gifts that have enabled me to complete this challenge and for carefully crafting the sequence of unlikely events that put me together with my coauthors in order to make this happen. And to Vitold Chraznoski, thank you for your constant support and mentorship in my walk with the Lord.

My most special thanks is to my parents for their constant support, wisdom, guidance and friendship. If, when I have children of my own, I can do even half as well in raising children, I would consider it a tremendous success. To the rest of my family, thank you for your interest and support, even when you have no idea what I am talking about and my actions seem to make no sense at all.

To Jillian Manus and Theresa Van Eeghan of Manuslit and Associates, your belief in our project and willingness to work with us helping us turn a wonkish manuscript into something that can make a difference in the world has been invaluable.

Bill U'Ren. Your editing skills are masterful and without you, even I wouldn't want to read the book.

To the Shorey PR Team – any chance of this book being a success is, in no small measure, due to your work. Roy & Missy, you are an incredible part of my journey on this book and in my life. It has been an entertaining ride and would never be what it is without you.

BearingPoint. To Carey Miller, Gordon Hannah, and Heather Gatewood, thank you for standing by as this trek proceeded and giving me the opportunities to develop my knowledge and skills in Privacy and Identity Management.

To Mary Dixon and Frank Jones of the Defense Manpower Data Center (DMDC), the opportunity you have given me to lead the DoD SSN Reduction efforts was a leap of faith and I can only hope that my efforts continue to be worthy of that trust. DMDC is one area of the Federal government where the status quo is never good enough. DMDC does more to push the bounds of and promote Identity Management than anywhere else in the Federal government. It is an exciting place to work and I am privileged to be a part of it.

Betsy Broder, Naomi Lefkovitz, Pavneet Singh, and everyone in the Identity Protection and Privacy Division of the Federal Trade Commission, thank you for the opportunity to kibitz on issues such as the Red Flags Rule, authentication and the President's Task Force on Identity Theft. Without the work that you do, this book would truly be about a nightmare.

In his book *Outliers*, Malcolm Gladwell writes about success never being a singular phenomenon. This book in clear proof that without a large cast of characters, success is not possible. To Mary Glynn Fischer, thank you for introducing me to John. Jim Povec, thank you for helping me to figure out that this is something that I should be doing. Lee Wingfield and Chris Nasbe, thank you for being guinea pigs and speaking the truth about the book, even when it hurt. And to John & Terry, Mike & Rupal, Mark & Jeannie, and many others, thank you for always asking about the book and keeping me on task. This book is for all of you.

Jeffrey and Rock, you are unbelievably patient with me and I am extremely grateful for everything you do in taking care of so many of the details. Without you and your work, this book would never have gotten off the ground.

John and Elizabeth, how does one thank someone for giving of their soul beyond measure? In everything from the rules of success to "connecting the dots," you opened my eyes to worlds that I had no concept of and challenged me to grow beyond what I knew to be possible. John's ability to put the pieces together of what Identity Theft is and why it matters and then to be able to translate that knowledge into something other than an academic exercise is unlike anything I have ever seen. Almost every time that I have brought new perspective to my work in the government, it is because of something that John has figured out and pieced together. Elizabeth, your ability to bring John and I back to the reality of what is important to our readers rather than our flights of fancy is the glue that makes this work. Your tolerance for my random calls distracting John from family matters is amazing. I could not ask for better, more powerful mentors.

Jeffrey Omtvedt

Thank you to my wife and son for providing me with unwavering support and for putting up with me during this process.

Thank you to my mom, dad, brother and the rest of my family for always encouraging me and instilling in me the desire to never settle and to do great things.

Thank you to my co-authors for allowing me to be a part of this fantastic journey and for constantly pushing me to reach the next level.

Thank you to my Lord and Savior, Jesus Christ, for loving me before I even knew You.

Contents

Introduction

Through the Looking Glass

Did you ever try to put yourself in Alice's shoes as she blundered her way around Wonderland? It was probably pretty frustrating and confusing. How would you like trying to figure out why nothing is what it seems and wondering if you'll ever find your way back to the world as you know it? Welcome to the reality of Identity Theft.

If you were to believe all of the advertisements, Identity Theft would only be about credit cards — "You won't lose any money, and for a few dollars a month you can totally protect yourself from it." Unfortunately, just as with Alice, the world isn't what it seems, and this conclusion would be dead wrong.

The story doesn't end there. What lies below Wonderland is even more reason to be concerned, and it shows us why Alice's chaotic journey is an appropriate analogy. When you gaze into the looking glass like Alice, what will you see? Hopefully, it's an image that closely resembles you. The insidious part about Identity Theft is that it can change what you see in the mirror, and it may affect you in ways that you probably can't imagine and may find difficult to believe.

The fact is that you are defined by a few numbers, most notably those on your Social Security card and Driver's License, and while these are the very things that make life so convenient, they also provide thieves the opportunity to use your good name to help them in ways that will hurt you in ways you couldn't conceive. And, contrary to popular opinion, the threat of Identity Theft isn't just about credit cards. In fact, its scope is only limited by the imagination of the thieves. That means that anything you can do in your name, someone else can do, too. Despite the old saying that "money makes the world go around," there are people who want things other than money, and your identity may just be what they need to help them get it all.

How Deep is the Rabbit Hole?

To paraphrase Baron von Rothschild, when blood is running in the streets there is massive opportunity. This is true both for the thieves and for the people who are offering solutions. And while there is nothing you can do to totally prevent becoming a victim of Identity Theft, there are a lot of things that you can do, by yourself or with help, to reduce your risk, decrease your likelihood of becoming a victim, and limit the damage that can be done to you or your family.

To accomplish all of that, we will help you to connect the dots walking through what the problem really is, the potential consequences to you, and your options for dealing with it. There are a number of steps, and each is an important part of helping you see beyond the looking glass to find your way out of Wonderland.

So if Identity Theft isn't just about credit cards, what is it really? If you ask a woman in Utah, the answer to that question might surprise you. Several months after having her purse stolen, she got a strange call from a social worker who said her infant child had tested positive for methamphetamine and the state planned to take the kid away, along with the rest of her children. It was true that the woman had more children, but the youngest was already several years old. The thief had actually used the woman's identity to receive medical care at a hospital during the birth of a child, which now was registered in the victim's name. To top it off, after the woman was finally able to prove that the record in her name belonged to a different person altogether, she still was denied access to the record because it wasn't hers, even though it was in her name and attached to her medical record. In addition to problems with the Department of Social Services, she received bills from the hospital that were not hers, and she continues to worry about her medical records containing inaccurate information.

We will walk you through all the types of Identity Theft, what they are, what they aren't, and how they may affect you. Make no mistake, this book is not the definitive work. More types of Identity Theft will appear as criminals become more creative and the crime transforms.

Beyond the crime are the people who are trying to help you. Some of their solutions are do it yourself and some are not. The catch is, where a problem demands a quick fix, a quick fix appears. In the words of Scott McNealy, Chairman of Sun Microsystems, "Many of the people in the protection business are making noises that look like they are protecting us, without actually providing any protection." 1 This is true from the policymakers down to the companies selling us products or services.

There are a number of products that have hit the market in the last year or so that claim to be able to totally prevent Identity Theft. The provider of at least one of these products is in trouble. This company has several class action lawsuits against it for not really living up to its marketing claims, one of which is of particular interest. A woman had her identity stolen, and the thief took a step that, while somewhat humorous to outsiders, nonetheless represents a serious concern. The woman who stole her identity signed up for an Identity Theft prevention service. The thief filed a fraud alert and set up a password which locked the victim out of her own identity. While the service isn't as good as it claims to be, the damage was still significant. Not surprisingly, the victim is now suing the company. This is far from the only thing that makes Identity Theft resemble Wonderland. We see commercials with a balding construction worker sounding like a ditsy teenager girl, or little old ladies sounding like rough bikers, making Identity Theft sound like a joke. We see a victim make the lead story of *America's Most Wanted*, portrayed on TV as a murderer even though she's a different race, five inches shorter, and fifty pounds lighter than the actual perpetrator. These stories seem to make a farce of Identity Theft, but the truth is that such cases should make you more concerned about the "protection" you are getting, not less.

As we walk through the things you can do to protect yourself, we will cover the whole range of options. There is quite a lot that you can do on your own, without spending a dime. Many tips are even available online. The Federal Trade Commission (FTC), the agency responsible for fighting Identity Theft, provides some of the best recommendations. The State of California also has some good suggestions. We have summarized most of what they offer, as well as some more advanced tips. With regard to the help you can pay for, we cover that, too. There are a whole host of products available to you, and it's important to understand the strengths and weaknesses of each type. Of course, there is no product that can totally prevent you from becoming a victim nor is there any product that can ensure that in every circumstance your identity can be restored, but we absolutely will recommend what we feel is the best protection you can get.

Individuals aren't the only ones at risk. Identity Theft for businesses is an important piece in connecting the dots, too. If you are in business, you may want to pay particular attention to this section. If you aren't, you may find this section a bit dry, but if you're up to it, you'll find out what's really being done by the government and others to help stop the pandemic from getting worse.

Businesses are increasingly likely to become victims of Identity Theft. They likewise face the significant risk of data loss. A great example of what business Identity Theft might look like is the case against ChoicePoint from 2004. A "company" signed up to receive services from ChoicePoint, asking for significant information on hundreds thousand individuals. Whatever fraud prevention program they had in place was clearly insufficient, because they provided the service, including information on more than 250,000 people. The fallout of this was severe, and ChoicePoint was taken to court by the FTC, resulting in a $15 million judgment. ChoicePoint has done much trying to clean up its act since then, but the fact remains that pretending to be a company can be as great a problem as pretending to be an individual, and the law is beginning to recognize this.

In addition to potentially becoming a victim, businesses are also at risk because almost every case of Identity Theft involves another organization (business, government, non-profit, etc.) along the way. The laws are beginning to hold all of them accountable. And they should, since more than half of Identity Theft is the result of information that came from such an organization. Not only are organizations now responsible for doing more to help prevent Identity Theft, they are increasingly being held accountable when they fail to prevent it.

Taken together, the situation could look bleak. And we are the first ones to say that parts of this book may read like a horror story (all the scarier since it is real). But we invite you to consider this: ignoring the problem doesn't make it go away. By walking you through this important material, presented in what we hope is a fairly entertaining manner, we believe you will be better able to understand and limit your risk. You will know what you can do, before and after, and you will understand why this problem isn't going away anytime soon. And by the end of the book, you will know as much or more about Identity Theft as most of the "experts."

IDENTITY THEFT FOR SOCCER MOMS

What is Identity Theft? This section is meant to reveal to the millions of Americans out there who are in the daily grind, making ends meet and making sure that their families are living as best they can. Our intention is to take a very complex subject and break it down so that you don't need to study for years to understand this terrible crime and why you should care about it.

How Many DUIs Have You Had?
Driver's License Identity Theft

So what's the big deal about a fake ID? You can find them at any college for a few dollars, right? But what happens when these IDs are used for something other than buying beer or getting into a bar? Trust us, you really don't want to find out the hard way!

Imagine you're returning home late one Saturday night after a visit with your parents. Your two children have fallen asleep in their car seats and you can finally relax. You hang up the phone with your husband who is returning home from a week-long business trip. Needless to say, you're excited to see him. It was a rough week, and you are both tired.

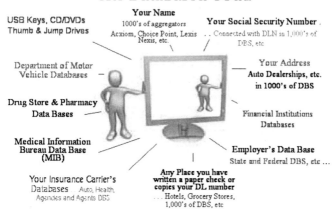

Your Driver's License Identity and The DataBased You ™

USB Keys, CD/DVDs
Thumb & Jump Drives

Your Name
1000's of aggregators
Acxiom, Choice Point, Lexis
Nexis, etc.

Your Social Security Number .
. . Connected with DLN in 1,000's of
DBS, etc

Department of Motor
Vehicle Databases

Your Address
Auto Dealerships, etc.
in 1000's of DBS

Drug Store & Pharmacy
Data Bases

Financial Institutions
Databases

Medical Information
Bureau Data Base
(MIB)

Employer's Data Base
State and Federal DBS, etc ...

Your Insurance Carrier's
Databases Auto, Health,
Agencies and Agents DBS

Any Place you have
written a paper check or
copies your DL number
... Hotels, Grocery Stores,
1,000's of DBS, etc

You are startled back to reality when you hear a loud siren and see flashing red lights behind you. As you slow down to let the officer pass, he slows down with you. Dazed a bit, you pull over to the side of the road. You can't believe you were speeding . . . and this is certainly not how you want the week to end. Your pulse rate has skyrocketed, and you haven't been this nervous in a long time.

The officer politely asks for your driver's license and registration and says you really *were* speeding. After a brief conversation, he realizes your situation and becomes sympathetic. Since you don't seem to pose a threat to anyone, he decides to let you off with a warning as long as "things check out." You sigh in relief as the officer walks back to his car. What could have been a disappointing end to a tiring week seems to be averted, and your heart rate begins returning to normal.

Suddenly, you are blinded by a spotlight behind you. The officer's blaring voice demands that you immediately step out of the car and place your hands on the hood. Your mind goes blank. The color drains from your face, and you can't move. The voice again commands you to step out of the car . . . slowly. Your children are now awake and crying.

As you cautiously open your car door and turn toward the white light of the police cruiser, you see the shadow of a gun pointing straight at you. The officer sharply orders you to stop and put your hands on the hood. Is this the same man who was so courteous only moments before? Your kids are now screaming as the officer approaches your frozen body and kicks your feet apart.

> You are allowed only to call your attorney, but whom do you call?

You still have no idea what is going on as he places handcuffs on your wrists and searches you. Tears run down your face, but you manage to ask the officer, "What is going on?" He looks at you quizzically and says, "What do you mean? There's a bench warrant for your arrest for DUI."

You are stunned. You've had only two tickets in your life, the last one of which was more than five years ago -- and, to top it off, both were for speeding . . . NOT DUI! When you explain this to him, he laughs and responds, "Everyone says that." The patrolman also tells you that another officer will be there momentarily to take your children to Family and Children's Services, while you'll be heading across town to jail. You are speechless. The nightmare is real!

By the time you reach the police station, you've convinced the officer you've been telling the truth, but his hands are now tied. They let your husband know what is happening. He rushes to the station, but there isn't much he can do, either. He isn't allowed to see you, and he can't even retrieve your children until morning. You are allowed only to call your attorney, but whom do you call?

After a brief court appearance, you are released on bail. The nightmare is over . . . for now. In reality, the nightmare is just beginning. You must hire an attorney to defend you from something you didn't do. In the meantime, your driver's license has been taken away, and you are expected back in court in a week.

As the days go by, through exhaustive research and the assistance of a private investigator, you begin to find out what happened. Six months ago, a woman was stopped for allegedly driving under the influence of alcohol. When asked for her driver's license, she handed the police officer a license with your name and number. The woman was released and scheduled for court, but she failed to show up on her appointed date. As a result, a warrant for *your* immediate arrest was issued. Since the alleged DUI took place months ago, you are left with the challenge of proving you were not the person at the wheel. This is the only crime in America where you truly are guilty until proven innocent!

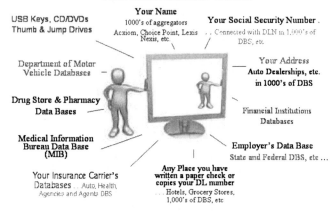

Your Driver's License Identity and The DataBased You ™

USB Keys, CD/DVDs Thumb & Jump Drives

Your Name
1000's of aggregators
Acxiom, Choice Point, Lexis Nexis, etc.

Your Social Security Number .
. . Connected with DLN in 1,000's of DBS, etc.

Department of Motor Vehicle Databases

Drug Store & Pharmacy Data Bases

Medical Information Bureau Data Base (MIB)

Your Insurance Carrier's Databases . . Auto, Health, Agencies and Agents DBS

Any Place you have written a paper check or copies your DL number . . . Hotels, Grocery Stores, 1,000's of DBS, etc

Your Address
Auto Dealers, etc. in 1000's of DBS

Financial Institutions Databases

Employer's Data Base State and Federal DBS, etc . . .

Your day in court arrives, and thankfully, it is short. Because you are an effective planner and keeper of records, you are able to "retrace your steps" via your calendar. You find that you were attending a church function on the night in question. You are also able to review the record of the arrest and prove the car the impersonator was driving is not yours. The officer who conducted the imposter's field sobriety test captured it on video, and although it was impossible to tell exactly who the woman was, the footage is clear enough to show she out-weighed you by at least 75 pounds and was no less than six inches taller than you. Your attorney is able to get all charges dropped, but your criminal re-

> This is the only crime in America where you truly are guilty until proven innocent!

cord will forever show you were arrested and tried for DUI. Let me repeat that – your name never comes out of the data-bases. There is no process to allow that to happen. It quickly becomes apparent that the difference between the person who commits a crime and the person who is framed for one is virtually nonexistent. You have also been fortunate that you worked for a small, family-owned business whose leaders were flexible and generous in giving you time off to respond to legal, judicial, and family issues.

The financial issues, however, have lasting effects. The costs for defending the drunk driving charges were not covered by your auto insurance, and the attorney's fees were high, so you were forced to take a large chunk of money from your IRA. And if you are ever stopped by a police officer in the future, you will always have to expect a different reaction when they see that dropped DUI charge on your record.

Does the above saga seem far-fetched? How about an 82-year-old grandmother in Rockville, Maryland who quit driving during the Truman administration. In 2001, she suddenly found herself in what she described as "a living hell"

> Your criminal record will forever show that you were arrested for DUI.

after one of her neighbors, arrested on drunk-driving charges in Illinois following a four-car collision, pretended to be her ... "I was told there were warrants out for my arrest... I was afraid to answer the phone".[2] A woman who had not driven in over half a century received a warrant for DUI. Think Driver's License Identity Theft can't happen to you? Think again.

In 2005, a fake commercial driver's license scheme was broken up in Florida. The ring included several members of the state license bureau who specialized in selling the false licenses to illegal immigrants. A number of the people who had been issued the fake licenses as part of this scheme had outstanding warrants as a result of their driving.[3]

So, How Does Someone Get Your Driver's License Information?

People can obtain your driver's license information very easily. Have you ever gone to a bar where they check IDs? Many bars and casinos use scanners to read the information off of IDs to prove that they are authentic. It is just as easy to *capture* the information as it is to read it. Have you ever test-driven a car or rented an apartment? Auto dealers are required to make a copy of your driver's license, and apartment leasing offices often do the same. Have you ever written a check and been asked for your driver's license number and absentmindedly watched the clerk jot it down on the check? Do you know for sure what they do with your information after you leave the premises? Are you confident the people who copied the information didn't make an extra copy for themselves?

When individuals obtain this information, what can they do with it? While most states have incorporated significant security programs to protect licenses from forgery, many of these programs have been compromised. State officials are concerned that they are unable to determine whether licenses from other states are legitimate. To help alleviate this problem, the Federal Government compiled a reference book that contains all states' driver's license security features.

Within a very short period of time, however, this supposedly secure book was available on e-Bay -- allowing potential identity thieves to know as much as state officials about driver's license security features. Thieves also determined that the best way not to get caught with a fraudulent driver's license is to "get caught" with the real thing. In fact, a few ingenious thieves in Nevada broke into a DMV office and stole computers, printers, and the raw materials needed to make as many "real" driver's licenses as they could sell.

When all else fails, thieves obtain licenses issued through the proper channels. In Miami, a ring of criminals, including several DMV officials, were apprehended for issuing commercial driver's licenses to illegal immigrants. Although the grand total number of these false licenses could not be confirmed, more than 50 of the individuals who possessed these fakes received traffic violations or were involved in traffic accidents. One individual was wanted for vehicular manslaughter as a result of an accident he caused. How would you prove that you aren't the you that they you are looking for?

> If you are ever charged with a crime resulting from an auto accident, don't look to your insurance company to help.

Speaking of vehicular manslaughter, this is one gaping hole in your auto insurance that most people don't know about. If you are ever charged with a crime resulting from an auto accident, don't look to your insurance company to help. You may want to examine your policy, but we haven't found any auto policies that will cover you in the event that this happens. Identity Theft or not, you are on your own. Think it can't happen to you? When was the last time that you got distracted while driving? It only takes a second, and whether you are looking back to check on your children, taking a bite from a sandwich, or talking on a cell phone, your life will change in an instant. While these examples don't have to be about Identity Theft, they also underscore why someone might want to use another name should it happen to them.

Driver's License Identity Theft may not be the most prevalent type of Identity Theft, but it is nonetheless a real threat. Like some of the other types of Identity Theft we explore in this book, it doesn't even make it on most people's radars.

Driver's licenses are the *de facto* National ID. That your driver's license number alone is worth $150 at the flea market should help you understand that it is being stolen to be used by others as an ID for driving, for work, even for medical treatment.

Action Steps

Now that you know what we know, here's what you can do!

- Limit the exposure of your Driver's License Identity. For example, don't pre-print the number on your checks.

- If your number is requested when buying goods, ask if they will accept the purchase without it. Remember: there is no law saying that you have to give this information to them. However, there is also no law saying they have to do business with you if you don't.

- Obtain a copy of your driver's record by contacting your local Department of Motor Vehicles. The cost is between $1 and $10, depending on the state in which you reside. Ensure that the records are accurate.

- When given a form to fill out requesting your driver's license number – don't fill it in. For instance, at your doctor's office, they will have a place for your Social Security Number, Driver's License Number, and Insurance Number. Do not ask whether you must give it; they will always say, "Yes." Just leave that part of the form blank. In our experience, they simply don't look. If they REALLY need it, they will let you know.

- If a business asks for your license and makes a copy of it, ask (loudly if others are present) if they are aware that the copier keeps a digital copy and what are they going to do about it. Since anywhere from 20,000 to 300,000 pages copied will go out the door with the copier, you should make sure that they have a plan to destroy the hard drive before getting rid of the copier. The law requires it.

Do You Know How Much You Made Last Year?
Social Security Identity Theft

Social Security Numbers are everywhere. Many people have started to question why they're being asked for SSNs every time they turn around (though many more still don't). Most often when we think of someone taking it to cause us harm, we think about credit cards and loans. We forget that SSNs were created for a real purpose. They're still used to track Social Security and taxes, and it is just as easy to misuse your number for that as it is for anything else.

It's a lovely spring day in the middle of May, and you're wondering when you'll receive your income tax refund in the mail. You did, after all, file your tax return by the April 15 deadline. In fact, you've already made plans for how you'll spend the money. You'll put some of it into savings, and the rest will go toward a splendid weekend getaway in Napa Valley. When you do finally receive correspondence from the Internal Revenue Service, it isn't at all what you were expecting. Rather than a check, you get a letter stating that you still owe more than $5,000 in Federal income taxes. It also states that you're now subject to an IRS audit because you filed your return improperly.

Your Social Security Identity and The DataBased You™

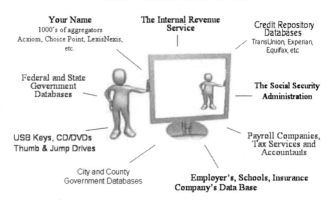

Your Name
1000's of aggregators
Acxiom, Choice Point, LexisNexis,
etc.

The Internal Revenue Service

Credit Repository
Databases
TransUnion, Experian,
Equifax, etc.

Federal and State
Government
Databases

The Social Security Administration

USB Keys, CD/DVDs
Thumb & Jump Drives

Payroll Companies,
Tax Services and
Accountants

City and County
Government Databases

Employer's, Schools, Insurance Company's Data Base

It must be a mistake, you claim. There is no way you added the figures incorrectly -- in fact, your tax software re-checked every calculation before you finalized and mailed the return. Because you received the letter on Friday, you are forced to wait until Monday before you can call the IRS to attempt to clear things up.

In the meantime, you decide to have a wonderful dinner on Saturday evening and discover that your debit card is rejected by the restaurant. When you contact the IRS on Monday morning, you are told there is no mistake. Your accounts have been frozen until you pay your back taxes, and all the arguing in the world isn't going to change the fact that they believe you owe this money. Nothing will be released until you pay up!

So, what can you do? While you know you don't owe the IRS any money, you also don't have access to any money to obtain the legal resources you need to help you prove them wrong. Fortunately, you are able to go to your parents for help. They give you enough money to buy needed groceries and retain an attorney.

As your attorney digs, he discovers that the IRS records show you reported income in three states from seven jobs. In two of the jobs, the proper amount of taxes was paid. In the remaining five jobs (all of which were reported as 1099 income), however, no taxes were paid. As your lawyer continues to dig, he also finds out that your Social Security Number (SSN) was used by illegal immigrants for these five jobs so they could obtain employment.

Your Social Security Identity and The DataBased You ™

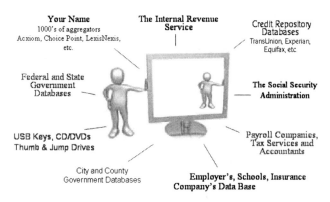

Your Name
1000's of aggregators
Acxiom, Choice Point, LexisNexis,
etc.

The Internal Revenue Service

Credit Repository Databases
TransUnion, Experian, Equifax, etc

Federal and State Government Databases

The Social Security Administration

USB Keys, CD/DVDs
Thumb & Jump Drives

Payroll Companies, Tax Services and Accountants

City and County Government Databases

Employer's, Schools, Insurance Company's Data Base

Fortunately, your attorney was able to produce sufficient details and evidence to prove to the IRS that this income was not associated with you. As a result, the IRS removed the freeze on your accounts and issued that income tax refund you were counting on. Unfortunately, you spent a significant amount of money and time—nearly $15,000 as well as more than two weeks of vacation (100+ hours) — to clear your name and remove the original $5,000 lien. Also, an IRS lien is now shown as having been filed in your name.

Think the IRS won't freeze your accounts or put a lien on your finances? The IRS placed a lien for more than $15,000 on the accounts of one victim as the result of his identity being stolen.[4] It's a Catch-22: you have to prove that you don't owe them the money, but you can't use your money to do it.

Do you believe the previous scenario can't happen to you? We're familiar with a woman who applied for a job at Target only to discover she'd already *worked* there. As she dug further, she found that 37 other people were using her SSN[5]. Unbelievable, you say? This may sound like a lot, but we've heard of cases much worse.

One might ask why the IRS wouldn't "catch on" to the use of one SSN for a number of different jobs. It's not uncommon for people to have two or three jobs—particularly when many of us have been advised to have multiple streams of income. If we do, then it makes sense that we'd "report" them. In partial defense of the IRS, how can it know which income reports are legitimate and which are cases of Identity Theft?

The use of stolen SSNs by illegal immigrants has become increasingly common, and recently-passed laws are causing the problem to grow worse. Employers are now required to verify the SSNs of all new employees. Because illegal immigrants either need or want employment, they are forced to obtain a SSN. In some cases, they act maliciously to obtain one, but often they acquire a SSN fraudulently without even knowing it. They may be convinced by their friends and/or family members that an assigned SSN was obtained legally, and so they don't even realize they are committing a crime.

A number of SSN scams exist, as well. One in particular involves a company that hires a group of workers for a contractual assignment. Each submits the required information to run payroll checks against the SSNs. After the employees cash the checks, nearly a month goes by before the checks are returned to the bank. When they are returned, the bank discovers that the SSN and the individual to whom the check was made payable do not match. In other words, the SSN does not belong to the payee.

A few examples of how this might look: a Caucasian male uses an SSN assigned to an African-American female, or a 40-year-old male uses a SSN that was assigned to a 15-year-old boy. We have heard of groups of workers coming in with false SSNs. Following the SSN match, the entire group is dismissed by the employer, and another group is hired with the same results. The cycle continues as the first group returns with brand new SSNs. We have heard countless examples of business owners who employ illegal immigrants (the only work force that some of them can get) who routinely change their SSNs to be able to work or even just to be able to cash checks. When the results come back with a mismatch, they have to change their SSNs to keep going. They also change their SSN to be able to cash checks. In this manner, a reasonably-sized group of illegal immigrants can go through an incredible amount of SSNs.

Two other examples: one of the co-author's most vivid experiences is of talking to a 75 year old man who had waited until age 72 to draw Social Security only to discover that someone had been receiving his checks since he turned 62. The Social Security Administration would not give him the higher amount for having waited. The other incident involved an attorney who told us he was representing a client who had his Social Security disability checks cut off. The Social Security Administration was demanding the disabled person repay all funds because the disabled person did not claim that he was working in another state (a thief was reporting the income). It took more than a year to get the matter straightened out — which probably went this quickly because he hired an attorney.

Some cases also involve an entire family that used the same SSN on job applications for each family member. And while they may only be doing what they need to survive, the effects on the person whose number they are using may be catastrophic.

So why don't the IRS and the Social Security Administration (SSA) do something to stop this from happening? First, the IRS and SSA hardly have adequate resources to investigate each questionable situation, and even if they did, they have fewer resources for stopping it. And, unbelievably, it is not in the best interest of either agency to stop these scams. While we would never in a million years suggest that either the SSA or the IRS would knowingly go along with any fraudulent activity, the Social Security is over $15 trillion in debt[6], and accepts deductions for Social Security from every paycheck it can. Even though it might collect 37 checks that originated from a single SSN, it will be required to issue only one Social Security check down the road for that SSN. The only person hurt may be you. The IRS and SSA have their work cut out for them trying to fix this problem.

To make matters worse, it is not always apparent a scam is even occurring. We mentioned earlier in the book that it may be very legitimate that a single person with a single SSN may be working for more than one employer, thus justifying multiple checks against the same SSN. If three incomes are reported under a single SSN, is it worth checking out? What about four? Where do you draw the line, and how can you be sure misuse is a reality?

It would be unfair to say that the government isn't interested in fixing the problem, but the scope of the issue is mind boggling. The 9/11 Commission and the subsequent Intelligence Reform and Terrorism Prevention Act of 2004 recommended that the Social Security Administration work to improve the security of the Social Security card. A cost estimate of this alone came in at more than $9 billion[7]. Unfortunately, this still wouldn't solve the problem. Think about it. When was the last time you used your Social Security card? Even when they do decide to replace the SSN (they are, in fact, working on it), the change will be incredibly expensive to implement.

The problem related to illegal immigrants isn't going away, either. We aren't trying to take sides. We just want to point out some important considerations. This is the first time we see the problems related to the Law of Unintended Consequences. In such scenarios, one action is taken and it results in side effects no one anticipated. By strengthening the legal requirements for getting work, the government has created a much greater need for SSNs, resulting in an even bigger market for your stolen information.

It really is a Catch-22 situation. Employers, in many cases, cannot find enough low cost labor, and to meet the requirement for verification of legal status of workers they put a copy of an SSN or Driver's License Number into the employee's file. One of the co-authors was speaking to a national meeting of risk managers from a particular industry whose workforce is approximately 90% immigrant-based. Up until two years ago, they would send in I-9 forms (Federal forms documenting proof of identity). They would occasionally get a mismatch letter back from the Social Security Administration noting a discrepancy between the name and the number and that the employee needed to go to the local SSA office to resolve it. The employer would put a note in the employee's file indicating the employee had been notified. With that, the matter was considered settled.

Today, it is a different matter because illegal immigration has become such a politically charged topic. When employers receive notice of a mismatch now, they have to release the employee (we'll call him Joe). Joe then leaves and returns as John (with new numbers) the next day. Since the business needs the work to get done (and figures it isn't really hurting anyone since the taxes are being paid) Joe/John is back at work. Again, the Law of Unintended Consequences is at work. Coming up with a solution to this problem is really going to be about figuring out which is the lesser of the evils that we face here.

Remember: being careful about using your SSN will help stop more than just issues with credit cards and bank accounts. While the IRS isn't really your enemy, they are used to being hated and lied to, and we can guarantee that they will be hard to convince should you become the victim of SSN Identity Theft.

Action Steps

Now that you know what we know, here's what you can do!

- The Social Security Administration (SSA) mails an annual statement to workers 25 and over. You'll receive yours approximately three months before your birthday. Be sure to review it carefully to make sure all your earnings have been reported. Inaccurate reporting now could affect the amount of the benefits you collect later. However, if you don't want to wait, you can contact the SSA and request a copy anytime at no charge. www.ssa.gov 800.772.1213

- When you get your statement, if there are earnings from places where you do not work, immediately have an attorney write a letter to the thief and his/her employer to stop using your SSN and/or name.

- If you become aware of problems resulting from someone using your SSN, you may have recourse against the business allowing someone to use your number to work. Contact an attorney and ask about possible remedies.

- The IRS has recently implemented an Identity Theft Tracking system to help prevent Identity Theft with your taxes. Should you become a victim of Identity Theft (tax related or not), call the IRS Identity Theft Hotline, 1-800-908-4490 to report it. For more information on this new protection system, please go to http://www.irs.gov/pub/foia/ig/spder/pipds-10-1008-02.pdf.

A Crime That Can Kill You
Medical Identity Theft

Money is money, but your health is irreplaceable. Unfortunately, there are a number of people who want to keep both at your expense. For many of you, this sounds almost surreal, but the truth here is very real, and finding out that it has happened won't be very much fun.

Imagine you and your family, after a stressful week, sitting around the dinner table discussing the "killer" plans you've made for the three-day holiday weekend. It's been over a year since you've all gone away for a few days to rest and relax. During the lively conversation, your husband's eyes glaze over and a strange look surfaces on his face. You ask if anything is wrong, but he shakes his head and picks up his fork to continue eating. A few

> **Money is money, but your health is irreplaceable.**

minutes later, he grimaces, and, in anticipation of your question, he mutters, "Darned indigestion." Finally, he admits his chest is tight and his left arm is numb. Your husband is having a heart attack.

The paramedics arrive, stabilize him, and load him into the ambulance. After enlisting the support of neighbors to keep an eye on your children, you follow in your car. When you enter the Emergency Room, you experience "standing room only" in a chaotic waiting area. Nonetheless, you make it to the "admitting desk" to begin the lengthy process of answering medical background questions, turning over insurance cards, and completing the waiver and consent forms.

As soon as the paperwork is completed, you are guided to your husband's intake room. On your way, however, an ER physician and nurse ask if you'd join them in a semi-quiet corner. They explain that your husband has been rushed into surgery and they are unsure about his prognosis. Although he was stable when he arrived, his condition changed quickly thereafter.

The doctor adds that your husband's diabetes and the fact that he is HIV positive certainly complicate the matter. You are completely surprised and blurt out, "But he doesn't have diabetes and he isn't HIV positive!" Equally surprised, the doctor asks your name again to ensure you are, in fact, the woman married to the man having surgery right now, which you confirm. The doctor explains that the medical records were pulled while your husband was in transit to the hospital and clearly include a previous diagnosis of diabetes and a record of regular insulin injections. The records also include an HIV positive diagnosis from almost two years ago. His course of treatment has been based on that information.

Fortunately, the doctor takes your word, for the moment, and rushes off to stop his current treatment in light of this new information. You are left to wonder and worry whether they can reverse the effects of the efforts the doctors have made acting on the wrong information. Forty minutes later, the doctor reappears and reports that your husband is out of surgery and in recovery. He will be transferred to the Intensive Care Unit, but his prognosis is good. He goes on to say he is thankful for the updated health information . . . if they hadn't had this information, it could have proven fatal. In a state of confusion, you ask how this could have happened. The doctor recommends that you call your husband's doctor and insurance provider to seek information about what is going on with his records.

After several days in the hospital, your husband is released to recuperate. What you fail to realize at the moment is that while one set of challenges is nearing an end, another set is just getting started.

Your Medical Identity and The DataBased You ™

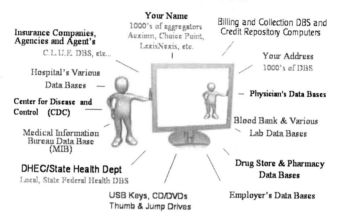

As you begin your investigation, you discover that insurance company records list your husband as having had three years of insulin treatment, along with a positive HIV test taken two years earlier. Although this test was performed in another state, no red flags were raised. Patients often test elsewhere to help ensure anonymity in their own communities. Since the insurance company is not allowed to cancel the policy due to your HIV status, no notice was ever sent.

You ask your husband about the premium payments and whether increases had occurred. He confirms steady increases over time, but he assumed these jumps in premiums were due to the rising costs of healthcare.

When he visits his physician's office, the news is even worse. Most records are paper (vs. electronic). While the office complies with all regulatory and insurance reporting requirements, staff members don't typically bother to verify the accuracy of receipt or any other patient information kept by these bodies.

They did not know about your husband's medical record inaccuracies and they are unsure how they happened or how they can be fixed. You consider hiring an investigator and/or an attorney to remedy things, but where do they start? Would it be possible to access *all* of your husband's medical records, including each place where the information went? Can they find the individual who actually had these diabetes treatments and that HIV test? Can they restore your husband's medical history to its original condition?

You learn along the way that accessing and correcting medical records is almost as difficult as getting your criminal history changed (which is basically impossible). This seems strange to you and your husband; you wonder why he can't just get a new physical examination so that a physician or clinic can revise the records accordingly. But it's not that easy. The holders of your records have no obligation to correct **anything**, and in most cases they are VERY reluctant to remove mistakes, particularly if they indicate services that have been rendered to the wrong patient.[8]

Your attorney suggests that your husband request a signed letter from his doctor stating that his medical record is inaccurate. The attorney further advises both you and your husband to keep a copy of the letter with you at all times.

Your Medical Identity and
The DataBased You ™

Your Name
1000's of aggregators
Aexiom, Choice Point,
LexisNexis, etc.

Insurance Companies, Agencies and Agent's
C.L.U.E. DBS, etc...

Hospital's Various Data Bases —

Center for Disease and Control (CDC)

Medical Information Bureau Data Base (MIB)

DHEC/State Health Dept
Local, State Federal Health DBS

Billing and Collection DBS and Credit Repository Computers

Your Address
1000's of DBS

— **Physician's Data Bases**

Blood Bank & Various Lab Data Bases

Drug Store & Pharmacy Data Bases

Employer's Data Bases

USB Keys, CD/DVDs
Thumb & Jump Drives

A year later, your attorney is able to report that she has completed her work. The inaccurate entries in your medical record are no longer associated with your name, but she advises you to check your records at periodic intervals to ensure they stay that way. She shares that it is not uncommon for similar inaccuracies to reappear. Unfortunately, the attorney was right. During one of your routine checks (almost six months after all corrections were made), the erroneous information showed up again on your husband's record. After three more months of tedious attention and a few hundred more hours, your attorney finally reports a "clean bill of health" for all records.

Does this story alarm you a bit? You certainly wouldn't be alone if you considered the above scenario unlikely. In fact, critics were skeptical when they suggested in an article in the September 2005 issue of *Money* magazine that one of our co-authors was exaggerating the possible consequences of Identity Theft, stating that Medical Identity Theft could kill you, or "[a]t least that's what a smooth talking southern lawyer by the name of John Gardner would have you believe."

Less than a year later, the attitude in the market began to change. The World Privacy Forum released a white paper in May 2006 entitled, *Medical Identity Theft: The Information Crime that can Kill You*[9]. And from September, 2006 to January, 2007, Medical Identity Theft was featured as a cover story for *Reader's Digest, AARP The Magazine, Consumers Digest, The Los Angeles Times, BusinessWeek*, and the *ABA Journal*. The general public is beginning to realize Identity Theft is a serious risk and can't be taken lightly.

Still not convinced? Here are some examples of additional cases:

- Just after getting shoulder surgery, a retired California school teacher started receiving calls from hospital bill collectors demanding that she pay for the amputation of her right foot. She was quoted, "Either you didn't do the surgery, or you did a really [shoddy] job of it." The reason: she still had both of her feet.[10]

- In California, a mother checked her mentally ill son's explanation of benefits to find that Medicare had been billed for more than 70 respiratory treatments, even though her son did not have a respiratory condition.[11]

- Victims in Southern California were given medical tests by non-physicians and had false diagnoses inserted into their medical files by a sophisticated, organized network of medical imaging companies. The individuals, according to an indictment, actively recruited Medicare beneficiaries with the promise of free transportation, food, and medical care. The perpetrators, posing as doctors and health professionals, obtained the victim's personal information and photocopied the victim's Medicare cards. The operation raked in $909,000 using victims' personal and insurance information.[12]

What Steps are Being Taken to Prevent Medical Record Inaccuracies?

The Health Information Portability and Administration Act (HIPAA) was enacted to regulate and protect the privacy of your medical information, but in some ways it also is being misused to protect fraudulent activity associated with records. Someone can visit the Emergency Room, for example, and identify himself as you. When the admitting clerk pulls up the record and compares the information (a 42-year-old Asian male) to the patient (a 25-ish Caucasian male), she clearly sees a discrepancy but proceeds anyway. If asked about it later by anyone other than her supervisor, the admitting clerk may not comment. Why? Because HIPAA training for employees dealing with medical information generally includes strong requirements not to disclose any medical information about patients or employees to others.

It can be even more frustrating if you determine that information in your name is not yours, and you are able to prove it, you are then often denied access to that information because it isn't you. The result is that you can't see the information to correct it. In October 2008, the Department of Health & Human Services held a town hall meeting to discuss Medical Identity Theft, and this very issue was raised. One of the panelists, a lawyer, stated she believed that according to the law you should be entitled to view the record. The fact that the record is in your name makes it so you are entitled to see it. Besides, for the person who got the health care to complain, they would have to admit to the fraud -- probably not very likely[13]

> If you determine that information in your name is not yours, and you are able to prove it, you are then often denied access to that information, because it isn't you.

Healthcare officials believe the creation of the National Health Information Network (NHIN) will have a significant impact on Medical Identity Theft. It is either entertaining or frustrating that the NHIN is about the only thing on which both Democrats and Republicans agree. Under the NHIN, every American's medical record would be maintained online. This idea gains greater attention because the network could save Americans billions of dollars each year. With the troubled economy and the fact that "[c]urrent estimates put U.S. health care spending at approximately 16%"[14] of Gross Domestic Product (GDP), any chances to cut significant costs are being aggressively sought. With costs continuing to rise, the savings from NHIN could be enormous.

While significant savings may be possible with NHIN, serious potential problems exist, as well. When medical records are digitized, they are easier to access. This may allow you to review your records periodically, but it also allows for more opportunities for misuse and Identity Theft. Records administrators and information system consultants are working diligently to ensure the safety of these records, but adopting these internal controls will take time, money and resources. And since converting the paper to digital means reading doctors' handwriting, what do you think the likelihood is that the records will be accurately transcribed? So the verdict is still out on whether this initiative will help the problem or make it much worse.

Medical Identity Theft, perhaps more than other types of Identity Theft, has the most serious consequences. In other types, you may lose time or money, and you may even be subject to prison, but Medical Identity Theft really could kill you.

Action Steps

Now that you know what we know, here's what you can do!

- Closely review the Explanation of Benefits notices sent by insurance carriers to ensure that services stated are accurate. The difficulty with this is that most notices are cryptic with diagnostic and procedure codes used by billing offices that most consumers will not understand, and not all insurance companies provide them. If you do receive them, make sure you take the time to read them carefully to understand exactly what is being documented.

- Pull your medical information bureau (MIB) profile and check for errors. The cost is $9. Call 617.426.3660 or visit www.mib.com.

- You may have legal remedies if the medical provider did not make reasonable efforts to confirm the identity of the person to whom they provided the medical services.

- Keeping an eye on your Credit Report will help when the criminals don't pay the medical related bill. The delinquent bill may show up as an outstanding debt.

It Wasn't Me, I Swear!
Character Identity Theft

Turn the TV channel to any crime drama and you will see suspects claiming they're innocent. Ask any judge or police officer and they will tell you the same: everyone says they're innocent. The reality is very few people admit that they actually did it! So, what happens when you really didn't do it?

You and your family have a long-standing tradition of getting together on the first Saturday evening of each month to enjoy "family game night." You and your 24-year-old son are wrapped up in a fiercely-competitive video game. Suddenly, you're interrupted by loud banging on the front door and voices shouting, "Police! Open up!" When you fail to answer the front door within 15 seconds, officers break it down and swarm in.

> Someone is out there committing crimes and using your name in the process.

The male members of your family are wrestled to the floor and handcuffed. A lead officer asks for John Williams to identify himself. When you do so, she explains that you are under arrest for an afternoon convenience store robbery. You are read your Miranda rights and taken to jail. After a confusing and uncomfortable night, you are arraigned and released on bail.

As your attorney investigates, he learns that the police were operating in light of an important piece of evidence found at the scene: a wallet which contained a driver's license, several credit cards, and a gym membership card. When the driver's license was shown to the convenience store clerk, she positively identified the person in the picture as the person who robbed the store. Although the person in the picture resembles you, he most certainly *isn't* you. Officers also based their arrest on film taken from the store's surveillance cameras. This time, the thief resembles you quite a bit!

Fortunately, however, the abundant sets of fingerprints taken from the scene don't match yours. One set, however, matches an individual in the criminal record system who was convicted of robbing several other convenience stores and is suspected of two carjackings, and unfortunately, that individual's record contains your name!

As officials continue their records search, they find that this individual has been using your identity for some time. He holds both an out-of-state driver's license and credit cards in your name -- even though your credit monitoring service has never detected inappropriate activity. In the end, you are cleared because the fingerprints found at the scene don't match yours and because you had an alibi. Nonetheless, you are left with a big problem.

Someone is out there committing crimes and using your name in the process. Your name, Driver's License Number and Social Security Number are now linked to fingerprints that are not yours. In the end, even though the culprit has been caught, your name has become one of his identified aliases. Every now and again, you will be forced to prove to authorities that you are not this criminal.

The Real World

<u>Example 1</u>—Though the circumstances in this story worked out, not every story turns out well. In one scenario, the Chief Operating Officer of a conservative women's group became famous, or at least achieved notoriety, when his name and identity were

> Even though the innocent man was a different race, height and weight than the criminal, he is forced to carry a letter issued by U.S. Marshals that explains the issue in the event he is ever questioned.

featured on the television program, *America's Most Wanted*. A criminal had assumed his identity and committed several crimes (including murder) in his name -- leaving the innocent man to be pursued by authorities. After years of work trying to clear his name and despite the fact that the innocent man was a different race, height and weight than the criminal, he is forced to carry a letter signed by U.S. Marshalls that explains the issue in the event he is ever questioned.[15] Like most other databases containing information about you, there is little chance of getting the information removed as no one thought to include this capability when they were being built. Now it is cost prohibitive to even think about adding that capability.

Example 2—Through a circumstance of Department of Motor Vehicles (DMV) Identity Theft, a woman was arrested 18 times for Driving Under the Influence (DUI) even though she hadn't driven a car since Harry Truman was president. Obviously, the first ten arrests weren't enough to make the point. Once the problem is on the books, it is tough to correct[16] This is also a good example of a case of Identity Theft covering multiple areas.

Your Character/Criminal Identity and The DataBased You™

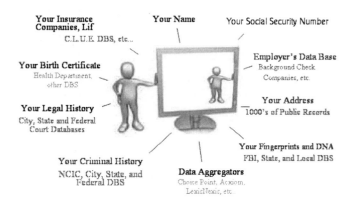

Your Insurance Companies, Lif
C.L.U.E. DBS, etc...

Your Name

Your Social Security Number

Your Birth Certificate
Health Department, other DBS

Employer's Data Base
Background Check Companies, etc.

Your Legal History
City, State and Federal Court Databases

Your Address
1000's of Public Records

Your Fingerprints and DNA
FBI, State, and Local DBS

Your Criminal History
NCIC, City, State, and Federal DBS

Data Aggregators
Choice Point, Acxiom, LexisNexis, etc.

Example 3—A nurse was mistakenly arrested as a drug-dealing stripper in front of her two children. As if that wasn't bad enough, her mug shot was included in a montage of gang members covered by the local media. Eventually, the charges were dropped, but there was no subsequent correction in the media. Anyone in town who had viewed the montage would think she was guilty. Ironically, the same police unit that arrested her had previously used a real person's identity for one of their agents to pose as a nude dancer.[17]

Example 4—One group that often commits Identity Theft (based on statistics) is sexual predators. After a conviction, they naturally want to fly "under the radar." Upon their release from prison, every single offender must register with a national database and report where s/he is living. Because sex offenders are likely to be ostracized or hassled and will probably have difficulty finding work, it may be much easier for them to "disappear." A perfect way to do this is to become someone else. And while these offenders probably won't care about the consequences of your name being associated with their perverse crimes, you will.[18]

In the 1990s, Landmark Entertainment operated several websites containing adult material and was eventually raided by authorities for dealing in child pornography. When police searched financial records, thousands of names from more than 10 countries came up. As the investigation progressed, a number of arrests were made. Somehow, members of the press learned about the raids and arrests, and they reported them. Many of those arrested were eventually found innocent -- either their credit card information had been used fraudulently or they had purchased legal pornography products from the company.

Although the law makes distinctions between legal and illegal products and services, the company was not so accommodating. Police found it difficult to determine whether purchasers had accessed legal pornography or child pornography. While many of these individuals were exonerated, their release and innocence never garnered as much attention in the media as their arrests. Many people lost credibility, jobs, homes, and families. More than 20 people even committed suicide. [19]

Unfortunately, the smearing of innocent victims happens much too often. Though it may not be as dramatic as the above example, nabbing suspects is far more dramatic and sensational than admitting a mistake was made. Prosecutors and police are often anxious to garner attention for doing their jobs (particularly when they are popularly elected), which only makes it more difficult for wrongly accused victims to clear their names.

Example 5—Do you have a security clearance for your place of employment? If so, and someone commits a crime in your name, you could lose this clearance. This has actually taken place! And in some instances, it has led to job loss. Given that it may take more than a year to get a security clearance and that the process may cost your company thousands of dollars, your bosses may not be happy when a crime shows up in your name that you didn't report.

Here's the catch: If you are unaware of a crime, you have no reason to report one. And since you signed a statement to obtain your clearance that you haven't committed any crimes, you are caught in a lie. Even if the issue is eventually straightened out, you face a difficult road ahead.

Some of you may not need a security clearance, but are bound to a professional code of ethics. Others of you may be required to undergo a background check. If your name is involved in anything inappropriate, you may face problems and/or be prevented from receiving licensures, clearances, jobs, etc.

Example 6—The following story, above all others, especially strikes a nerve with the authors. A police officer was in the process of booking a suspect for a misdemeanor, and as part of the process, requested the suspect's SSN. The suspect stated a number, and the officer stopped cold in his tracks. He asked the suspect to repeat his SSN. After the suspect's reply, the officer shared in a raised voice, "That is NOT your number, and where did you get it?!"

The criminal assured the officer this was indeed his SSN. Finally, in an outrage, the officer demanded the suspect to tell him where he got the number. Why? Because it was the officer's SSN![20]

Clearing Your Name?

How tough do you believe it is to clear your records after a crime has been committed in your name? Your challenge isn't only ensuring that authorities acknowledge you are not a criminal. Once inaccurate information is in the records, it has a great likelihood of popping up again and again and is difficult to straighten out.

Your Character/Criminal Identity and The DataBased You ™

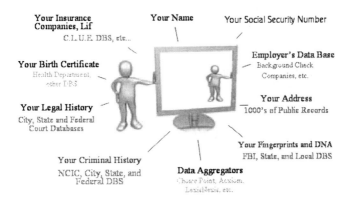

To answer the question about how difficult it may be to clear your name, let's ask another question. How many people who are on trial enter the court room and claim their innocence? In the movie, *The Shawshank Redemption*, Morgan Freeman's character "Red" probably said it best, "Everybody in here is innocent."

An article about Character Identity Theft that appeared in *Kiplinger's*[21] October 2005 issue indicated that courts are skeptical of defendants who claim to be victims of Character Identity Theft. Even *if* a judge believes your story, however, the FTC reports, "[o]nce your name has been recorded in a criminal database, it's unlikely that it will be completely removed from the official record."[22]

The effects of Character Identity Theft are so cliché as to be almost funny. But when it happens to you, it is anything but. Saying "It wasn't me!" probably won't be enough.

Action Steps

Now that you know what we know, here's what you can do!

- There really aren't any good actions to take to help prevent this specific crime from happening. And the only way you are likely to find out it has happened is when you are denied a job or picked up for an outstanding warrant.

- Filing an Impersonation Report with the local police may be a good step to take if it happens to you.

- Some states have Identity Theft Passports. These are actual documents issued to confirm the identity of victims. If you are a victim and have such a passport, you should carry it with you at all times.

- If Identity Theft Passports are not available in your state, carry a notarized/certified copy of the Court Order clearing your name. If there is an outstanding warrant for your arrest for failure to appear in court, you are going to want one in one hand and your attorney on the phone in the other when you are stopped by the police.

The Commercials May Be Funny, But The Crime Isn't Financial Identity Theft

While the subject of this chapter needs little introduction -- it's the one form of Identity Theft that we've all heard of -- it still may not be what you think it is, and it almost certainly is more than you think it should be. While this form of theft can be the easiest to fix, that doesn't mean the resolution process will be completely painless.

You are a divorced single mother struggling hard to make ends meet. You work two jobs trying to pay your bills. Your ex-husband is always late with child support payments. You live in an apartment barely big enough for you and your two children. Since you got married shortly after finishing high school, you never had a chance to develop a credit history of your own; everything was in your husband's name. The credit card that you have has a very low limit, which you don't mind, because you pay it off every month. Although you would like to build up your credit rating, you are not interested in building up debt. You have seen what debt can do and you have no intention of getting into financial trouble.

Since you have been paying off your credit card every month, with no late payments for more than a year, you feel ready to get another one. When you apply for the new card, you are declined. You ask for more information, and they send you a summary of your outstanding debts. You discover that you have two other credit cards with different billing addresses, there is a car loan in your name with late payments, and a house that you supposedly bought is now in foreclosure. You are stunned. The car you're driving has been paid off for at least two years and you don't own a home. You want to know how this happened and what you can do to fix it.

Your Financial Identity and
The DataBased You ™

The credit cards are the simplest problem to deal with, but they still are not exactly "easy" fixes. You have coverage for any fraudulent charges that happen to your existing accounts, but not on new accounts opened in your name. You are eventually able to get the banks to eat a few of the charges, but they try to recoup some of their money by charging it back to the retailers. You are now faced with several retail establishments pursuing you in civil cases for their losses.

The car loan is not so easy to fix, either. The finance company didn't do a check on your credit beforehand, and now they've already tried to repossess the car in question. Since they obviously weren't able to find you with the vehicle, they have begun to harass you to get their money. The fact that the company specializes in high-risk loans only makes it worse and they are relentless in coming after you.

The house foreclosure is the most surprising item on the list. Oddly enough, the thief provided a significant down payment, enough to convince the bank that you were operating in good faith. The large down payment allowed the loan size to be decreased into an amount you could've been expected to pay monthly. Unfortunately, the thief took the equity created by the down payment and the increased property value resulting from a fraudulent appraisal as part of a home equity loan. Shortly after the equity was withdrawn, the normal mortgage payments stopped. The house was moved to foreclosure two months ago.

You are now faced with one bank, one auto finance company and several merchants working hard to get every dime they can from you. They are relentless. Although the commercials make finance companies look like they are your friends, they really are kind of like guard dogs. They can be warm and friendly at times, but when it comes down to it, they can tear the throat out of anyone who gets in the way. This is not to say that they are bad people or companies, but they have been around for years, and have seen countless people who claim that they don't owe any money, have repaid the money, or will pay it back shortly. How are they to determine whether you are telling the truth or not?

Unfortunately, this story doesn't have quite so happy an ending. You are eventually able to get most of the retailers to drop their claims, but the car and mortgage people aren't so accommodating. After more than a year, you still owe over a $100,000 to creditors.

If you think you can't lose money like this, think again. One of the more famous cases of Identity Theft was the subject of an in-depth CBS story. In approximately 4 months, an Identity Thief racked up over $260,000 worth of debt to a Connecticut salesman. After more than 2,000 hours (that is a full-time work year) he still owed nearly $145,000 to creditors. He had a letter signed by the Department of Justice that stated that the money had been taken by thieves and that he had not incurred the debt. That didn't matter to the creditors who still believed he owed them money.[23]

Another example involves a couple who discovered that someone had taken out a home loan in their name. They proved that this had happened and that they had never seen any of this money. This did not stop Homecomings (the company holding the loan) from coming after them. Homecomings sued the couple for the entire amount of the loan, claiming that the couple had done injury to Homecomings by not acting faster to prevent the fraud. In this case, things worked out in

> The FTC defines Identity Theft as "fraud committed or attempted using the identifying information of another person without permission."
>
> Regulation E is very specific in that it only allows individuals to be liable for $50 of fraudulent charges to existing credit card accounts. The same is not true for debit cards.

the end. The couple got the lawsuit dropped, but at a cost to themselves in time and money.[24]

A small business owner found out that $90,000 had been transferred from his bank account. He discovered it within hours of the transaction and reported it to authorities, including the Secret Service. They discovered a key logger virus on his computer. Bank of America claimed that he should have had more robust virus protection in place and refused to put back his money. The thieves were able to get away with this because the money was in an account that belonged to the business, not the individual. Since the account was not directly linked to an SSN, it was not protected by Regulation E.[25]

To take a step back, let's look at what qualifies as Identity Theft. This last case doesn't actually meet that standard. Credit card fraud and bank fraud are certainly terrible crimes, but they are distinct from Identity Theft. The FTC defines Identity Theft as "fraud committed or attempted using the identifying information of another person without permission."[26] Credit card fraud and bank fraud, for the most part, do not include this. Why is this important? The fact is that different laws govern these crimes, and you as an individual are much better protected than companies from credit card fraud and bank fraud. Regulation E is very specific in that it only allows individuals to be liable for $50 of fraudulent charges to existing credit card accounts. On bank or debit cards you are liable for $50 for the first 48 hours. After that, your liability goes up incrementally until 60 days, after which you are liable for the entire amount. If the thief has changed the address and you don't know about the debt until after the 60 days, you are still liable for the debt.[27]

Beyond the specifics we've just discussed, any fraud can cause problems. It affects millions of people every year. The problem has grown to the point that the revenue generated in the trafficking and misuse of your financial information surpassed that of drug trafficking in 2004.[28] While some of this may be from Identity Theft, most of it is not. The Identity Theft that tends to get you is less about actions taken to existing accounts and more about new accounts. This is definitely a lower percentage of the activity, but a much higher percentage of the damage. The crimes that really rack up the damages are loans taken out in your name, whether for a car or a home. Since a single loan can cost a lot more than a credit card bill, banks are far more likely to come after you for the loan. Also, in the case of the credit cards, the banks can always pass the bill back to the retailers. As the damages from these crimes continue to rise, this happens more and more often.

Your Financial Identity and
The DataBased You™

Your Name
1000's of aggregators
Acxiom, Choice Point,
LexisNexis, etc.

Social Security Number
used @ Auto Dealerships, Financial
Aide Offices, Employers, etc.

Your Real Estate Deeds
Clerks of Court DBS

Banks and Credit
Unions

Your Accountant, Financial
Planners and Third Party
Administrators.

Credit Card Companies
and Collection
Agencies

USB Keys, CD/DVDs
Thumb & Jump Drives

Mortgage Brokers and
Lenders

Your Credit History
Credit Repositories' DBS
TransUnion, Experian,
Equifax, etc.

Insurance Carriers

Data Aggregators
Choice Point, Acxiom,
LexisNexis, etc..

While you may be lucky enough to get out of Financial Identity Theft without owing any money, it is almost certain that the grueling remedy process will still cost you. It may be money, time or anxiety and stress, but you will pay. And when you're going through it, it most certainly won't feel like a victimless crime.

Action Steps

Now that you know what we know, here's what you can do!

- Get copies of your Credit Reports to help determine whether or not someone has opened accounts in your name. Credit monitoring is a fast way to have someone else check this for you.

- Opt out of credit mailings to reduce the amount of junk mail you receive. It can help reduce your risk of Identity Theft. You can register for the Do Not Mail list at: https://www.directmail.com/directory/mail_preference/

- Call your credit card company or bank if you don't receive your monthly bill. It may be a sign that someone has taken it or changed the address on your account.

- Check your statements each month, even if you don't use the credit or card and it has no balance. If someone else gets it and starts using it, you may not catch on if you aren't checking the account each month. AARP reported that thieves are now stealing just one card from your wallet or car, not taking the entire purse. If you aren't aware the card is gone, you won't know you've been hit.

Connecting the Dots

Isn't it amazing how you never seem to hear about all of these different areas of Identity Theft? The stories are out there, but until you see them all together, the severity of the problem isn't quite so apparent.

Since Identity Theft is only limited by the imagination of the thief, should it be surprising that there are so many types? We don't think so (although we are still occasionally intrigued at the lengths some people will go to commit these crimes). The fact is, we haven't seen them all yet. As the importance of Personally Identifying Information (PII) grows and is used for more and more things, thieves will continue to find new and creative ways to commit Identity Theft. One way that is starting to appear is called Synthetic Identity Theft. We haven't described it as a separate type here as it has more to do with how the false identity is created rather than the type of fraud committed.

Look at the five types of Identity Theft that we have outlined, so far:

Five Common Identity Types

Drivers License   Social Security   Medical   Character/ Criminal   Financial

People make decisions about you that are based on more than the information in your Credit Report.

It is imperative that your Personally Identifiable Information and your Non-Public Information be as protected and as accurate as possible.

The same information can be used to commit any and all of these crimes. This is important to understand because it hopefully should make you a bit more protective of where and to whom you give your information. Just because you give it to a bank doesn't mean that it can't end up being used at a hospital.

In a number of places in this section, you've probably noticed pictures of computers linked to databases underneath a reference to something called The DataBased You. The DataBased You is the sum total of all of the information out there about your life, compiled, aggregated, categorized, cataloged, sorted, stored, and sold across a multitude of databases. One magazine article put it this way, "Thanks to database technology that has become ever more pervasive, it can be aggregated and collated and turned into a startlingly comprehensive dossier on you in the blink of an eye."[29] The average American appears in at least 50 databases, not counting government files[30], and more than 86% of these are updated at least daily. Lee Tien, a Senior Staff Attorney with the Electronic Frontier Foundation, said, "There is something weird and creepy that these systems can build a better biography of me than I could myself."[31] This does not mean that there is a single file out there somewhere with some secret organization pulling your strings; it's actually much worse! Your grocer, your insurance company, your bank, your doctor, your boss, and a thousand other people all know something about you. Unfortunately, you have no control of who has that information and what they might do with it.

The DataBased You is made up of all types of data. On top of the basic demographic information (age, sex, income, martial status, address, date of birth), additional details are filled in by your purchasing behavior.

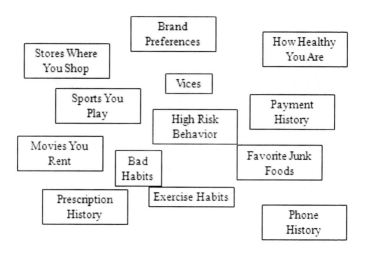

All of these and a thousand other details come together to make a portrait of who you are, or at least who the computers think you are.

The DataBased You is important because it is the basis for almost every decision made about you. The Police Officer doesn't care who you say you are, but who his computer says you are. The doctor believes your medical record, not you. The opinion of the IRS about you is based on what its computers say about you. And when an identity thief makes you a victim, the information in The DataBased You gets messed up. So decisions are being made about you based on information you know isn't right, which you can't access to refute or correct. When the thief gets a DUI in your name, it goes into a local database, then gets sent to the county, state, and finally to the Feds. Even if you get the record corrected at the local level, the incorrect information can resurface when the record gets updated -- replacing all the fixes you made. You could make correcting the misinformation about you into a full time career and still never fix it all.

Knowing that decisions made about you are generally based on what the computer says about you rather than what you say may be a bit disconcerting. It is doubtful that the situation will ever change back. But knowing what is happening may help in knowing what to do in the event that bad decisions are made about you because of inaccurate information. Start with the source of the information and work backwards. It may be a painful process, but it is likely to be the only way to fix the problem.

If you hire an attorney who doesn't normally work in the Identity Theft arena, and we only know a few, then make sure that they read this book so they have a starting point for what the damages to you may truly be and see how deep the Rabbit Hole goes.

The Web Of The DataBased You ™

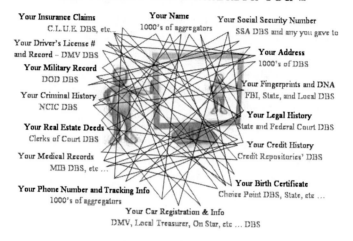

Your Insurance Claims
C.L.U.E. DBS, etc...

Your Name
1000's of aggregators

Your Social Security Number
SSA DBS and any you gave to

Your Driver's License #
and Record – DMV DBS

Your Military Record
DOD DBS

Your Address
1000's of DBS

Your Criminal History
NCIC DBS

Your Fingerprints and DNA
FBI, State, and Local DBS

Your Real Estate Deeds
Clerks of Court DBS

Your Legal History
State and Federal Court DBS

Your Medical Records
MIB DBS, etc ...

Your Credit History
Credit Repositories' DBS

Your Phone Number and Tracking Info
1000's of aggregators

Your Birth Certificate
Choice Point DBS, State, etc ...

Your Car Registration & Info
DMV, Local Treasurer, On Star, etc ... DBS

Your Identity as a Fixer-Upper Opportunity

This is not necessarily something you want to think about, but knowing what to do when it happens is better than being forced to find out *after* the fact. As you have seen in the previous chapters, there are many reasons why someone would want to take your identity. Given the ease with which such a crime can be committed, it truly is a matter of when you become a victim, not if. Knowing what to do may make the difference between whether the problem it causes is just a simple nuisance or a nightmare. And as with approaches to household maintenance and repair (you can do it yourself, hire an individual, or contract a service) many options for protecting and restoring your identity are available, too.

Not If, But When

Every book on Identity Theft has basic tips on what to do. But now that you understand that Identity Theft is about much more than just charges to your credit card, you can see more clearly why you should follow these recommendations. Knowing what can happen to you if you have your identity stolen is critical to learning why you need to protect your personal information and can then help you to figure out what you need to do.

Let's start by looking at your risk. The most important thing to remember is that you actually *are* at risk. It is time to accept this. Complete prevention of Identity Theft is impossible since you don't control all of your identity information. Because your information is stored in databases and used on a regular basis (by other people), it is extremely difficult to control who sees it and what those people do with it. Let's look at some examples of how that might happen.

The easiest way to understand our point is to ask a few questions. Do you maintain a bank account? Visit a doctor occasionally? Go to a gym?

> If you're in the system, then you are at risk of Identity Theft.

Own or rent a home or apartment? Own and/or drive a car? Vote? If you answered yes to any of these questions, you're in the "system." Do you have a Social Security Number? Are you employed anywhere? Do you pay for purchases with anything other than cash or use loyalty cards when you make purchases? Again, if the answer is yes, then you're in the "system." And if you're in the system, then you are at risk of Identity Theft. And if you aren't, well then life is probably hard enough already and Identity Theft is the least of your concerns.

Are there other risk factors? Well . . . do you have relatives or friends or neighbors? Do you have a mailbox? Do you have or use a computer? E-mail? A cell phone? If so, then you are at risk.

So, where is it safe? The answer is nowhere. But before you consider moving to a cave and becoming a hermit, let's at least look at ways to reduce your risk significantly.

The list of actions you can take to help reduce your risk is long. You may have heard about many of these ideas before, but some may be new to you. One of the best lists that you can follow comes from the FTC. They spend a lot of time working to help citizens solve this problem on their own. They also are the main Federal government point of contact for victims to submit complaints. That makes them the best positioned to put together a list of things you can do to help yourself. Here are some of the steps they recommend:

- Don't carry your SSN card; leave it in a secure place.

- Give out your SSN only when absolutely necessary, and ask to use other types of identifiers. If your state uses your SSN as your driver's license number, ask to substitute another number. Do the same if your health insurance company uses your SSN as your policy number. Another place where you may get asked for information is for your children at school.

- Carry only the identification information and credit/debit cards you'll actually need when you go out.

- Be cautious when responding to promotions. Identity thieves often create phony promotional offers in an attempt to seduce you into giving them your personal information.

- Keep your purse or wallet in a safe place at work; public buildings are a breeding ground for less-than-honorable individuals to scour the premises for unattended personal belongings . . . especially during the early morning and late afternoon hours as well as lunch time.

- Store all copies of administrative forms that contain your sensitive personal information in a safe location.

- When ordering new checks from the bank or credit union, pick them up from the facility rather than having them mailed to your home mailbox.

- To opt out of credit offers that come in the mail, call 1-888-5-OPTOUT (1-888-567-8688).

- Don't disclose personal information over the phone, through the mail, or on the Internet unless you've initiated the contact and/or you are sure you know who you're dealing with on the opposite end.

- Treat your mail and trash carefully. Tear or shred charge receipts, copies of credit applications, insurance forms, physicians' statements, personal checks and bank statements, expired charge cards, and credit offers you receive in the mail.

- Fight "phishing" – don't take the bait.

- Check your Credit Reports – for free.

- Check your bills and bank statements to ensure they are correct.

- Renew and upgrade your virus protection software on a regular basis.

- Download and install patches for your operation system and software programs that protect against intrusions and infections that could compromise files or passwords.

- Do not open files, click on hyperlinks, or download programs from people you don't know.

- Use a firewall program, especially if you use a high-speed Internet connection (like cable, DSL or T-1) that allows your computer to be connected to the Internet 24 hours a day.

- Use a secure browser – software that encrypts or scrambles information you send over the Internet – to guard your online transactions.

- Do not store financial information on your laptop unless absolutely necessary.

- Before you dispose of a computer, delete all of the personal information stored inside. The best way to do this is to physically destroy the hard drive.

- When making decisions about purchases via the web, review the website privacy policies before supplying any personal information or finalizing purchases.

The above ideas represent some of the basic steps you can take to reduce your risk of Identity Theft. But are there other actions you can take? Absolutely! Here are some advanced tips:

- When people ask for personal information, find out *why* they're asking. You may have noticed that many retailers now regularly request your phone number at the checkout register. Do you share this information when asked? In almost every case, they're asking to get some information about you for their database. There are compliance requirements regarding what they can ask for. They may say it is to make sure that you are who say you are, but in most cases it isn't.

- Reset the default passwords on all of your computers. This may seem simple, but may not be so easy. First, there are a large number of websites that publish the default passwords for virtually every tech device available. Second, you may not have found all of the places where your computers require passwords. If you don't know about it, how can you change it? Many companies who use Voice Over IP (VOIP) found out the hard way that their systems had back doors that they hadn't closed. Any criminal who had the default password was able to get in and have free reign of the system.[32] If you need assistance, your best bet may be to go to the computer store and ask the Help Desk. Other options may be to call the Help Desk for any software you may have installed.

- Are you the administrator of your own computer? Unless your computer has been provided to you by your employer, it is likely that you have administrative rights to your computer. This means that anytime your computer picks up a virus, it will be able to get anywhere in your computer. The best thing you can do is to create a login for yourself that doesn't use "admin" rights. Don't use these rights unless you need to. If you don't know how to do it, find a nearby teenager, they can do it for you.

- Don't trash old fax machines and copiers. They have hard drives that remember many of the things that have gone through them. When you do have to get rid of them, make sure that you pull out the hard drive and destroy it. And as nice as it is to give old computers to charity, the same is true here. Even if you delete the data, most savvy computer operators can get it all back! If you are really intent on giving away the computer with the old hard drive, take it to the computer store and ask their help in erasing it. The added protection to you is worth the cost.

- Don't fill in all of the blanks when people ask you for information. This is particularly true in the doctor's office. They often ask you for your SSN when all they really need is your Insurance Number.

Because Identity Theft is a continually evolving crime, and the places where they can get your information are as varied as the events of your life, the list of things to do to protect yourself is almost never-ending. For those people who think that the government should be able to pass a law and have the problem fixed, we would only suggest that theft has been around since the dawn of time, and we still haven't figured out how to stop it. Identity Theft is no different. It will be an ongoing battle by us and by the thieves to stay ahead of each other. So while our list of "fixes" is extensive, it is certainly not exhaustive, and as more come our way, we will be sure to pass them on to you.

We aren't suggesting that you need to live life as a paranoid. Doing so might severely reduce your risk, but who needs to live as a basketcase? Now that you

> We aren't suggesting that you need to live life as a paranoid.

know where most of your risk lies, you can take some simple steps on a regular basis to reduce the biggest piece of your risk.

The Do-It-Yourself Kit

Are you the type of person who likes to fix things yourself? If so, then this is the chapter for you. In excruciating detail you can see what to do about fixing your identity. But fixing your identity isn't quite the same as fixing a car. No matter how smart you are, there are probably some things you won't be able to do without some help.

The most important thing for you to know about this chapter is that no matter how you package this information, it may read like a textbook and certainly isn't humorous. Nor can we claim that much of this is our original thoughts. While it took quite a bit of time to compile and sort through the sources, almost all of the information we are presenting can be found freely online. In fact, the best way to bring it to you is give you information from the best government sources that originally did the work to develop these corrective steps. The most complete and important of these is the FTC guide *Take Charge: Fighting Back Against Identity Theft*. *Take Charge* is a free publication that can be ordered from the FTC website (www.ftc.gov/idetheft) or by phone (1-877-ID-THEFT). The other resource that has a pretty good list of actions to take is the California Division of Privacy. Their information can be found on their website (www.privacy.ca.gov). The following information is taken primarily from these two resources, with some additional comments by the authors. To make it easier to compare, you will find the sources presented side by side in columns, though in cases where the information is very similar, we haven't included the information from both. It is also important to note that all of this information is produced by the government and therefore is public domain and can be copied at will (this will be an important consideration in the next chapter).

When you discover you have become a victim...

File a Police Report

FTC Guide: *Take Charge*	California Division of Privacy
[G]et a copy of the police report or at the very least, [get] the number of the report. It can help you deal with creditors who need proof of the crime. If the police are reluctant to take your report, ask to file a "Miscellaneous Incidents" report, or try another jurisdiction, like your state police. You also can check with your state Attorney General's office to find out if state law requires the police to take reports for Identity Theft. Check the Blue Pages of your telephone directory for the phone number or check www.naag.org for a list of state Attorneys General.[33]	Under California law, you can report Identity Theft to your local police department. Ask the police to issue a police report of Identity Theft. Give the police as much information on the theft as possible. One way to do this is to provide copies of your Credit Reports showing the items related to Identity Theft. Black out other items not related to Identity Theft. Give the police any new evidence you collect to add to your report. Be sure to get a copy of your police report. You will need to give copies to creditors and the credit bureaus. For more information, see "Organizing Your Identity Theft Case" by the Identity Theft Resource Center, available at http://www.idtheftcenter.org/vg106.shtml.[34]

The tough thing about police reports is that many police departments are reluctant to take reports for Identity Theft. It is not a crime that they can prosecute, usually crosses multiple jurisdictions, and in general, they don't really know what to do about it. One thing that may change this is the President's Task Force on Identity Theft. One of their recommendations is to develop a standardized police report for Identity Theft. Until such time as this becomes available, you will just have to be persistent. Without the police report, many of the other steps become impossible.

Notify Credit Bureaus

FTC Guide: *Take Charge*	California Division of Privacy
	You can report the Identity Theft to all three of the major credit bureaus by calling any one of the toll-free fraud numbers below. You will reach an automated telephone system and you will not be able to speak to anyone at this time. The system will ask you to enter your Social Security number and other information to identify yourself. The automated system allows you to flag your file with a fraud alert at all three bureaus. This helps stop a thief from opening new accounts in your name. As a victim of Identity Theft, you will be sent a free copy of your Credit Report by each of the credit bureaus. Each report you receive will contain a telephone number you can call to speak to someone in the credit bureau's fraud department.
	Equifax 1-800-525-6285 Experian 1-888-397-3742 TransUnion 1-800-680-7289[35]

Hire an Attorney

Hiring an attorney is a step that appears in several places, but it is not one that rates a high place in either guide. That's because many of the things that need to be done can theoretically be done without the services of an attorney. We would disagree with their conclusion, as many of the actions require the use of an attorney, particularly the non-financial types of Identity Theft. There is no way that you will ever get your medical or criminal records changed without a lawyer, and there's still only a small chance even with one on your side. The question of what type of attorney to hire is a difficult question as it really depends on where you live, where the Identity Theft took place and what the thief did. It is important to find an attorney who specializes in the area and geographic location that is consistent with the crime. Again, not a simple problem, but one that can save you headaches going through the rest of the steps.

Contact All of Your Creditors

FTC Guide: *Take Charge*	California Division of Privacy
	Call creditors for any accounts that the thief opened or used. When you call, ask for the security or fraud department. Examples of creditors are credit card companies, other lenders, phone companies, other utility companies, and department stores. Tell them you are an Identity Theft victim. Ask them not to hold you responsible for *new accounts* opened by the thief. If your *existing credit accounts* have been used fraudulently, ask the credit issuers to close those accounts and to report them to credit bureaus as "closed at consumer's request." If you open a new account, have it set up to require a password or PIN to approve use. Don't use your mother's maiden name or the last four numbers of your Social Security Number as your password. Ask the creditors to give you copies of documentation on the fraudulent accounts (see above item). For more information on what to tell creditors, see the Federal Trade Commission's "When Bad Things Happen to Your Good Name," available at www.ftc.gov/bcp/conline/pubs/credit/idtheft.htm.

File A Complaint with the FTC

FTC Guide: *Take Charge*	California Division of Privacy
By sharing your Identity Theft complaint with the FTC, you will provide important information that can help law enforcement officials across the nation track down identity thieves and stop them. The FTC can refer victims' complaints to other government agencies and companies for further action, as well as investigate companies for violations of laws the agency enforces.[36]	

This is a really important step that many people fail to take. The best way that the crime of which you have been a victim can be linked to others by the same thief is through the FTC. They are the only ones equipped to receive and analyze the data and give you the best chance to see that criminal brought to justice. The FTC works with virtually all major law enforcement agencies to coordinate their efforts.

Initiate a Fraud Alert

FTC Guide: *Take Charge*	California Division of Privacy
Fraud alerts can help prevent an identity thief from opening any more accounts in your name. Contact the toll-free fraud number of any of the three consumer reporting companies below to place a fraud alert on your Credit Report. You only need to contact one of the three companies to place an alert. The company you call is required to contact the other two, which will place an alert on their versions of your report, too. • **Equifax:** 1-800-525-6285; www.equifax.com; P.O. Box 740241, Atlanta, GA 30374-0241 • **Experian:** 1-888-EXPERIAN (1-888-397-3742); www.experian.com; P.O. Box 9532, Allen, TX 75013 • **TransUnion:** 1-800-680-7289; www.transunion.com; Fraud Victim Assistance Division, P.O. Box 6790, Fullerton, CA 92834-6790	

Get Copies of Credit Reports

FTC Guide: *Take Charge*	California Division of Privacy
Once you place the fraud alert in your file, you're entitled to order free copies of your Credit Reports, and, if you ask, only the last four digits of your SSN will appear on your Credit Reports. Once you get your Credit Reports, review them carefully. Look for inquiries from companies you haven't contacted, accounts you didn't open, and debts on your accounts that you can't explain. Check to ensure that information like your SSN, address(es), name or initials, and employers are correct. If you find fraudulent or inaccurate information, get it removed. Continue to check your Credit Reports periodically, especially for the first year after you discover the Identity Theft, to make sure no new fraudulent activity has occurred.[37]	

Fraud alerts, credit freezes and credit monitoring are important topics and will be tools that can provide assistance for you as a victim, but they have significant drawbacks. Some of our concerns about their use are addressed later in the book.

Write To and Obtain Documents From Creditors

FTC Guide: *Take Charge*	California Division of Privacy
	Write a letter to each creditor where an account was opened or used in your name. Repeat what you said in your telephone call. Send a copy of your police report. Black out the account number of any accounts with other creditors on a copy of your completed ID Theft Affidavit and send it. Sample letters are available on our Identity Theft web page at http://www.privacy.ca.gov/cover/identitytheft.htm.[38]

Obtain Documents from Debt Collectors

FTC Guide: *Take Charge*	California Division of Privacy
	Tell the debt collector that you are the victim of Identity Theft. Say that you dispute the validity of the debt. Say that you did not create the debt and are not responsible for it. Send the collector a follow-up letter saying the same things. Include a copy of your police report and of any documents you've received from the creditor. Write in your letter that you are giving notice to a claimant under California Civil Code section 1798.93, subsection (c)(5) that a situation of Identity Theft exists. Send the letter by certified mail, return receipt requested. If the debt collector is not the original creditor, be sure to send your letter within 30 days of receiving the collector's first written demand for payment.

Block Information in Your File

FTC Guide: *Take Charge*	California Division of Privacy
Consumer reporting companies will block fraudulent information from appearing on your Credit Report if you take the following steps: Send them a copy of an Identity Theft report and a letter telling them what information is fraudulent. The letter also should state that the information does not relate to any transaction that you made or authorized. In addition, provide proof of your identity that may include your SSN, name, address, and other personal information requested by the consumer reporting company.	
The consumer reporting company has four business days to block the fraudulent information after accepting your Identity Theft report. It also must tell the information provider that it has blocked the information. The consumer reporting company may refuse to block the information or remove the block if, for example, you have not told the truth about your Identity Theft. If the consumer reporting company removes the block or refuses to place the block, it must let you know. [39]	

Treat All Papers as Evidence in a Criminal Case

For you to have a chance to get the person that did this to you, it is important for you to be able to show everything that you've done to try to correct the problem. Everything is important, and you had best keep records as though your life depended on it, because your good name may very well depend on how well you do this. Since you are far more interested in your case than anyone else, your records may be the best chance that law enforcement has to prosecute the criminal.

Chronology and Detailed Journal

Any story should have a thorough plot. The best way to make sure that your Identity Theft story is put together well is to make sure that its parts are all in the same place. If you take the time to use a journal, everything should be annotated. Every phone call, every letter, every action should be documented. This journal should be as thorough as you can make it. All of the letters, phone log, and receipts should be referenced here.

Any Proof of the Fraud

As you go through your investigation to clear your name and your identity you will find evidence. Make sure that you keep it. You will also need to show it to Law Enforcement so that you can get them to do more to help you. But even if you give the evidence to them, make sure that you have a copy of it. You should never give up any part of your case without keeping copies for yourself.

Credit Reports

FTC Guide: *Take Charge*	California Division of Privacy
	When you receive your Credit Reports, read them carefully. Look for accounts you don't recognize. Look in the inquiries section for names of creditors from whom you haven't requested credit. You may find some inquiries identified as "promotional." These occur when a company has gotten your name and address from a credit bureau to send you an offer of credit. Promotional inquiries are not signs of fraud. (By calling to report Identity Theft, your name will be automatically removed from the mailing list to receive unsolicited credit offers of this kind.) Also, as a general precaution, look in the personal information section to verify your Social Security number, address and name. If you find anything you don't understand, call the credit bureau at the telephone number listed on the report. Tell them you want to block, or remove, any information on the report that is the result of Identity Theft. (You must send a police report of Identity Theft to support this request.) Order new Credit Reports every three months or so until your situation has cleared up. You may have to pay $8 or $9 for each report, but ask for additional free copies as an Identity Theft victim. For more on what to tell the credit bureaus, see the Privacy Rights Clearinghouse's "Identity Theft: What to Do When It Happens to You" at www.privacyrights.org/fs/fs17a.htm.[40]

Credit Reports are valuable for more than just Financial Identity Theft. Evidence of other forms of Identity Theft may appear on them. Certainly many instances of Medical Identity Theft eventually appear on Credit Reports, normally after the thief has neglected to pay for the services. These become outstanding debts in your name.

Medical Records

Since there is no central repository for medical records, the task of correcting your medical records isn't as simple as cleaning up your Credit Report. On top of this, there is nothing that requires any medical provider to remove inaccurate information from your medical record. Medical providers are required to allow you to make amendments to your records, but there are significant restrictions and limits on making this happen. Neither the FTC Guide nor the California Privacy Division has anything that discusses how to make such amendments. Good resources for this include the Identity Theft Resource Center (http://www.idtheftcenter.org/index.html) and the World Privacy Forum (http://www.worldprivacyforum.org/index.html).

First, you need to ask your provider for access to or a copy of your record. With some exceptions or restrictions, you should be able to get it, though they are allowed to charge you a reasonable amount for copying the record.[41]

As mentioned in a previous chapter, you may have significant difficulty getting a copy of your record. If they claim that you aren't allowed to see it because it isn't your information, take it up with the Legal Department. You can argue that since the record is in your name, you are most certainly entitled to see it. A fundamental point of the privacy laws was to ensure transparency allowing you to see what the records say about you. It may take an attorney to make this point, though.

Having determined that inaccurate information is in your record, you can request an amendment to the record. Don't be surprised if you have a tough time proving your case.

While the people holding your record are required to amend inaccurate information, there isn't anything that really covers their criteria for accepting amendment requests. There are a number of exceptions and restrictions on amendments, many of which can make restoring your record nearly impossible. And since there is no standardized form for amendments, it may be difficult to notice when they have been made. The least valuable, but most common way is to make a note that the following information is inaccurate or is regarding another individual. Because your medical record is almost always the business record and the legal record for services provided, the record holder may be very reluctant or unwilling to delete the information. The best corrective measure we have heard of is where the inaccurate information is de-identified. That means that they keep the record of what services have been provided, but they create a separate record for the false information without any link to your name. This is the best of both worlds in that it protects the records and the provider while restoring your good name to the greatest extent possible. Hopefully more service providers will move toward this model until a better solution is found.

Even if you are able to get your record amended, your problem may not be over. For example, if the record is no longer in the hands of the entity that entered the inaccurate data, they have no obligation to correct it. While they must make reasonable efforts to inform others of the amendment (within a reasonable time), the burden of that effort will likely fall on your shoulders, since they get to determine what "reasonable" means.[42]

Just because your medical record is inaccurate doesn't mean that it was a case of Identity Theft. The coding/billing can often be the source of problems. The provider may charge you for something that belongs in another record or bill you for the wrong service. This is a case where "Garbage In, Garbage Out" may not be appropriate. It may be "Garbage In, Garbage Stays!"

Electronic Health Records may be coming, but until such time as they are available, the largest consolidation of medical records to date belongs to the Medical Information Bureau. While they do not have records on everyone, they do have many. To request a copy of your records from them, call 866-692-6901.

Criminal Violations

FTC Guide: *Take Charge*	California Division of Privacy
Procedures to correct your record within criminal justice databases can vary from state to state, and even from county to county. Some states have enacted laws with special procedures for Identity Theft victims to clear their names. You should check with the office of your state Attorney General, but you can use the following information as a general guide. If wrongful criminal violations are attributed to your name, contact the police or sheriff's department that originally arrested the person using your identity, or the court agency that issued the warrant for the arrest. File an impersonation report with the police/sheriff's department or the court, and confirm your identity: Ask the police department to take a full set of your fingerprints, photograph you, and make copies of your photo identification documents, like your driver's license, passport, or travel visa. To establish your innocence, ask the police to compare the prints and photographs with those of the imposter. If the arrest warrant is from a state or county other than where you live, ask your local police department to send the impersonation report to the police department in the jurisdiction where the arrest warrant, traffic citation, or criminal conviction originated. The law enforcement agency should then recall any warrants and issue a "clearance letter" or "certificate of release" (if you were arrested/booked). You'll need to keep this document with you at all times in case you're wrongly arrested again. Ask the law enforcement agency to file the record of the follow-up investigation establishing your innocence with the district attorney's (D.A.) office and/or court where the crime took place. This will result in an amended complaint. Once your name is recorded in a criminal database, it's unlikely that it will be completely removed from the official record. Ask that the "key name" or "primary name" be changed from your name to the imposter's name (or to "John Doe" if the imposter's true identity is not known), with your name noted as an alias.	

By changing the primary name on the record to that of the identity thief, you reduce the likelihood of your being subsequently arrested for the offense. When your name is run through the computer by someone checking, you are less likely to raise any flags if your name is only an alias.

FTC Guide: *Take Charge*	California Division of Privacy
You'll also want to clear your name in the court records. To do so, you'll need to determine which state law(s) will help you with this and how. If your state has no formal procedure for clearing your record, contact the D.A.'s office in the county where the case was originally prosecuted. Ask the D.A.'s office for the appropriate court records needed to clear your name. You may need to hire a criminal defense attorney to help you clear your name. Contact Legal Services in your state or your local bar association for help in finding an attorney. [43] Finally, contact your state Department of Motor Vehicles (DMV) to find out if your driver's license is being used by the identity thief. Ask that your files be flagged for possible fraud.	

Each state has a different way to locate the attorney you may need to help do it yourself. We wish we could provide you with a single place to go to find the one you need, but as far as we know, there isn't one.

Prosecutors and Victims

You may wish to mark a copy of this book and give it to investigators, attorneys and prosecutors to help educate them. The hardest thing for us to realize is that by the time that you finish reading this book, you will probably know more about this terrible crime than many of the "experts." Very few people understand that there is anything other than Financial Identity Theft. And even if they do know about the other categories, they don't spend much time speaking about them. We tend to take the opposite approach. We think that non-financial Identity Theft is harder to fix and has more serious consequences.

Driver's License

FTC Guide: *Take Charge*	California Division of Privacy
If you think your name or SSN is being used by an identity thief to get a driver's license or a non-driver's ID card, contact your state DMV. If your state uses your SSN as your driver's license number, ask to substitute another number.[44]	

The paragraph above may look very similar to the one in the previous section and there is a good reason for that. As you've no doubt figured out, many cases of Driver's License Identity Theft also show up as Criminal Identity Theft. And similar actions may be required for both. Another important point to consider is that you can't really check to see if you have a Driver's License in any other state. This could pose a problem for you.

Social Security Number Misuse

FTC Guide: *Take Charge*

Social Security Administration (SSA) – www.ssa.gov

If you have specific information of SSN misuse that involves the buying or selling of Social Security cards, may be related to terrorist activity, or is designed to obtain Social Security benefits, contact the SSA Office of the Inspector General. You may file a complaint online at www.socialsecurity.gov/oig, call toll-free: 1-800-269-0271, fax: 410-597-0118, or write: SSA Fraud Hotline, P.O. Box 17768, Baltimore, MD 21235.

You also may call SSA toll-free at 1-800-772-1213 to verify the accuracy of the earnings reported on your SSN, request a copy of your Social Security Statement, or get a replacement SSN card if yours is lost or stolen. Follow up in writing.

SSA publications:

• *SSA Fraud Hotline for Reporting Fraud* www.ssa.gov/oig/guidelin. htm

• *Social Security: Your Number and Card (SSA Pub. No. 05-10002)* www.ssa.gov/pubs/10002.html

• *Identity Theft And Your Social Security Number (SSA Pub. No. 05-10064)* www.ssa.gov/pubs/10064.html

Tax Fraud

Internal Revenue Service (IRS) – www.treas.gov/irs/ci

The IRS is responsible for administering and enforcing tax laws. Identity fraud may occur as it relates directly to your tax records. Visit www.irs.gov and type in the IRS key word "Identity Theft" for more information.

If you have an unresolved issue related to Identity Theft, or you have suffered or are about to suffer a significant hardship as a result of the administration of the tax laws, visit the IRS Taxpayer Advocate Service website www.irs.gov/advocate/ or call toll-free: 1-877-777-4778.

If you suspect or know of an individual or company that is not complying with the tax law, report it to the Internal Revenue Service Criminal Investigation Informant Hotline by calling toll-free: 1-800-829-0433 or visit www.irs.gov and type in the IRS key word "Tax Fraud."[45]

Telephone Records

This is one more piece to the puzzle. You should keep track of every call that you make as you attempt to restore your identity. Note the name of the person to whom you spoke, the time and date of the call, the substance of the call, and anything else that seems important. Not only does this help you with remembering what was said and what actions you've taken, it also accounts for calls that are included in the cost to you.

Costs

The only way that you can be reimbursed for expenses incurred is to know what you have spent. This includes phone calls, letters, affidavits, lawyers hired, and anything else that you may need in order to complete your investigation. If your insurer has a reimbursement policy (discussed in the next chapter) you need to be able to prove to them what you have spent.

Copies of All Letters Sent or Received

Copies of these letters are just one more piece of your overall records. Keep copies of every letter that you send as well as every response that you receive. It is particularly important that

> As you work to restore your identity, do not hold any illusions that it will be a simple or easy process.

the copies are of what you sent, including signatures, not just a soft copy of the letter (without your signature). Each letter and response should also be explained in your journal.

Court Documents

If any piece of your case goes before a court or arbiter, make sure that you have copies of everything that happens. This includes trial transcripts, motion rulings, or anything else that may show what happened regarding your case.

Victim Statements

Although your own statements may be important, this really means statements or affidavits from other victims of the same criminal. The point is to help build a case against the thief who took your identity.

Summary of Case to Date

As you move forward with the case, make sure that you document your thoughts and feelings. Your case is not just the facts. You have to make sure that if it comes before a court that they can see into how this made you feel -- how you felt as though you'd been violated, how you fought your way out of the hell that the criminal put you through. Sum up the facts and the conclusions you have drawn from them.

As you work to restore your identity, do not hold any illusions that it will be a simple or easy process. Also, do not think that just because you went through the process once, that you are finished. Unfortunately, many people find that once their identity has been taken, it is gone for good. Just because you stopped the person who took it the first time, doesn't mean that your information isn't still out there. Not only that, once bad items get put into your record, they seem to have a devious way of sticking around. A quick analogy, if you don't mind...

A few years ago, when airlines were still service providers, some friends of a guy, as a joke, decided to call the airline and tell them that their friend was a vegetarian. The first time that a flight attendant brought him a vegetarian meal, it was kind of funny. But when it showed up, the fifth and tenth time, it stopped being amusing. He called and wrote, and was given reassurances that the matter had been resolved. But every time that he flew, he received vegetarian meals. No matter

> Many people find that once their identity has been taken, it is gone for good.

what he did, the original joke didn't seem to go away. It took him more than 5 years to finally get it removed and to get the regular meal. This is a harmless example (unless you are the one getting the wrong meal), but it illustrates how bad things can keep coming back around in the world of Identity Theft. Sorry to rain on your parade, but we wouldn't want to feed you lies.

Good Guys Wear Black

With the problem of Identity Theft running amok, there are a host of people trying to tell you that they have the one and only solution. They present themselves as white knights rushing in to save you from the dragon. The problem is that amongst those people genuinely trying to help you, there are even more who want to take you for everything else. A quote from the Despair, Inc. website says it pretty well, "If you're not part of the solution, there is good money to be made in prolonging the problem."[46] The reality is that there is no single product that is a panacea. Your information is just too easy to get, and there are too many ways to misuse it. There is no way that a single remedy product can perform well in every area. The best way for you to determine what you're getting for your money (if you spend any) is to understand the weaknesses in the products as well as the strengths. Unfortunately, the gaps that you discover may turn your stomach, so be prepared.

> The question is not what is the best way to protect or restore your identity, but what is the right answer for you?

The best way to think about protecting your identity is to relate it to health care. Having health insurance is no guarantee that you won't get cancer and it is no guarantee that if you get cancer that you won't die. But having health insurance will likely give you a better chance to prevent it, to detect it early, and to cure it if you get it. But just as with health care, you have to treat the disease, not just the symptoms, and you had better be trying to cure the right disease.

There are free cures for Identity Theft, and there are cures that cost money. There are ongoing services, and there are one-time actions. There are advocates who say that you should never have to pay to have your identity restored, and there are those willing to pay any amount. There are so many different options that it can be very confusing. The question is not what is the best way to protect or restore your identity, but what is the right answer for you? Certainly, we have an idea about what we believe to be the best, most comprehensive answer, but you need to make up your mind for yourself. We just want to make sure that you are making an informed choice, rather than one that is based on the latest fad or the best sales pitch.

There Is No Such Thing as a Free Lunch!

The most popular option for Identity Theft protection and recovery is the do-it-yourself approach. There are a number of reasons for this. First, there is the very vocal group that shouts from the rafters that Identity Theft isn't your fault and that because you didn't do anything to cause it, you shouldn't have to pay anything to get it fixed. While this is great in an ideal world, most of us have to live in the real world. If you are mugged walking down the street, who is it that has to pay? Of course the answer is you. And by the way, if you think that businesses aren't paying for Identity Theft, think again. We are by no means saying that companies should be held blameless, but it should not all be laid at their feet.

The second group of people in this category feels that Identity Theft isn't that big of a deal and that they will have no problem fixing things themselves. And in the largest number of cases they are right (to some extent). They can fix it themselves. The questions you need to ask yourself are: how much work do you want to do, do you have the time to do it, and how much stress are you willing to endure? You read in the previous chapter what you have to do if you wish to do it yourself. You may luck out

> The questions you need to ask yourself are: how much work do you want to do, do you have the time to do it, and how much stress are you willing to endure?

and you may not have to go through all of the steps we showed you. But what if your luck doesn't hold up?

If you wish to have help working through the process of restoring your identity (otherwise known as learning the hard way how to become a lawyer), there are a plethora of free counselors, hot lines, websites, support groups and any manner of self-professed sages to tell you what to do. How good any of them are is anyone's guess. Certainly, some of the government-sponsored organizations have solid experience, but their ability to provide support may be directly affected by how many cases they handle. It's the same old story – lack of resources. Attorneys General are swamped, the FTC is underfunded, and law enforcement has other things that are a higher priority.

Just because there is no cost associated with the help that you get from these organizations, doesn't mean that you won't have to pay. According to Gartner, the average out-of-pocket expense to recover from ID theft was $3,257 in 2006, up from $1,408 in 2005[47]. Victims spend an average of 600 hours[48] recovering -- that is 15 40-hour work weeks. Nearly 25% of victims are never able to completely restore their identity.[49] We don't know about you, but that certainly doesn't seem like it's free to us.

Outsourcing

One of the biggest trends in business today is to outsource anything that you can. The world has continued to get faster and faster, and we have less time to do things that we aren't good at or that can better be done by specialists. Businesses have found that it is more effective and more efficient to hire another company to take care of areas that are beyond their expertise. Jim Collins, in his book *Good to Great*, discusses the idea of core business. Companies that succeed to the highest levels concentrate on the things that they are good at and outsource as many of the areas that are beyond that expertise as possible.[50] Many individuals do this, as well. You hire an accountant to do your taxes and a financial advisor to manage your money. You hire plumbers and electricians to fix your home. And you may even hire someone to clean your house because you don't have time to do it as well as they will.

If the description above makes sense, you really don't need us to tell you that you should have someone to watch your identity. The rest of this chapter involves you spending some money. You should understand what is available, even if you do not intend to buy.

> Businesses have found that it is more effective and more efficient to hire another company to take care of areas that are beyond their expertise.

The question you should now be asking is, if you're going to have someone watch out for your identity, what do you get? With so many choices, how can you tell which is the right product for you? And how do you get beyond the sales hype to find out what the products do and what falls under the fine print? The rest of the chapter is dedicated to a review of the product types that are available to you as a consumer. You will note that not a single product is named. We are looking at classes of products, not specific brands. Individual products will likely claim to not have many of the faults that we will point out, and they may be correct, but we think that you should see it in writing before you believe it.

Technology is the Answer?

How many times have you heard that technology is the cure for your problems? If you are like us, far too often. This is not to say that technology can't provide some significant protection for you. In fact, technology plays an integral role in Identity Theft protection. Even the people who don't believe in getting Identity Theft protection will most likely agree that you need to have up-to-date virus protection, anti-spyware, antispamware, and other products for your home computer. With all of the latest updates and software, you are still susceptible to the many nasty things that live on the Internet.

A previous technology innovation is also a good example of what can happen when a problem arises. Before 2000, it was pretty uncommon to find anyone using virus protection. Suddenly, the problem of viruses hit the public radar. Within 24 months, virtually everyone had protected his or her computer. Now, if you own a desktop or laptop, you couldn't imagine being without these anti-virus programs. Although there are some who would disagree, we think it is likely for the same type of result to happen regarding Identity Theft. The analogy of spyware and virus protection is especially poignant. We feel fairly certain that within the next few years, Identity Theft protection will be as much a requirement as virus protection or auto insurance.

The race to keep up to date with the latest protective technology is never-ending, and the criminals are generally at least one step ahead. Unfortunately, most of the problem lies in you, your home computer, and the two feet in between. Approximately 61% of all personal computers in the U.S. are compromised to some extent.[51] According to an expert from Microsoft, many of these programs may be difficult or even impossible to remove. He suggests that the only way to get rid of them is to "nuke it from orbit."[52] In other words, you have to totally remove everything from the computer and re-install the operating system, or, for the non-computer people, take it to a computer store and have them "re-image" it. This process is a major hassle, but it can save you tremendous heartache later on. Again, it would be nice if such extremes weren't necessary, but sometimes you don't really have much of a choice.

As to the technology solutions, there are a wide array of services available, but they operate in an online environment.

That means they protect your computer. They can't do anything to protect the information about you that is already out there and available. They can't prevent you from being the victim of a scam that happens when you work from other computers, and they can't stop you from being the victim of many types of scams, such as phishing. In other words, while the tech guys can do a lot to protect your computer, they can't do much to protect you from yourself.

We are not suggesting that technology products aren't important. In fact, we are big proponents of some of these services. But you have to know their limitations and their appropriate uses. Technology can help detect viruses and prevent spam. It can help you to tell who to trust and who to avoid online. What it can't do is stop you from falling prey to social engineering attacks. It also won't stop every thief that tries to come after you. In other words, it can be a help, but it is certainly not a panacea.

> You should understand what is available, even if you do not intend to buy.

Credit Monitoring

Powerful information tools at your disposal are credit monitoring and reporting agencies—the single, comprehensive repositories of virtually everything related to your financial identity. Because they allow you to receive instant access to credit and money, they are significant drivers of any economy. With centralization of this data, any suspicious financial activity relating to you can be monitored easily. While this is helpful to you as a consumer, it is also helpful to identity thieves. With all of the important financial data about you in one place, a thief with your information holds the key to your financial kingdom when he/she obtains access. So, the same tool that is your first line of protection is also your Achilles' heel.

If you find the above hard to believe, we invite you to take a closer look at the situation in Europe, where there are no central credit repositories and companies are not allowed to sell or transfer your personal information without your permission. As a result, many people believe the United States would be better off with the European model. There are pros and cons to both systems. The fact that there is no central repository for financial information means that the thieves can't do as much damage to your identity, but it also means that you have no way of knowing when a breach occurs. And if you don't know about it, you can't fix it. Europe is having as much difficulty with data loss as North America, but they're having much more difficulty finding out if anything has happened to people as a result of the losses.

Credit monitoring is a key protection in the United States because it allows consumers to find out when someone attempts to open a new account in their name—as long as providers check with the credit bureaus before authorizing credit. When searching for a monitoring and reporting service, are there characteristics you should look for? Absolutely. Why? Because all monitoring programs are not created equal.

We recommend a continuous monitoring program, which shortens the amount of time between someone inappropriately using your identity and you finding out about it. The more quickly you find out, the more easily it is to stop the misuse and minimize damage. If, for example, someone uses your name to purchase a car and you're able to visit the dealership within a few days, it is likely easier to prove you were not the person who bought the car. The longer the time between Identity Theft and your corrective actions, the less likely you are to be protected by law (we will discuss this in the next chapter).

Any monitoring program should start with a copy of your Credit Report. This allows you to see what's in your file and ensure you aren't a victim already. Some programs (particularly ones offered by credit cards) only cover specific pieces (such as activity on that specific card). If they offer just this, then they really are only protecting themselves, but giving you the privilege of paying for it.

One particularly important feature you should seek in a monitoring program is instant notification if someone changes your address for you. Although it is very complicated to change your address (go to the post office or a company like U-Haul, fill out a change of address form, and send it to the Post Office), some criminals might just be able to figure it out. You will get a notice in the mail, but if you are like most Americans, you probably don't open and carefully read every piece of mail you receive (especially if it doesn't seem to make sense or look important). If you miss that initial notification, you could be in serious trouble. Quick thieves can get what they need and change your address back before you've even noticed that it's happened. But if your monitoring service gives you immediate notice of a change, you can prevent fraud and save yourself some heartache. You also want to make sure that your monitoring service has an effective way to inform you that something has happened. The notification should stand out as important -- not just as one more piece of junk mail or another spam email. We also recommend that any monitoring program should let you know periodically that all is well (at the very least monthly). That way, you'll know that you haven't missed a report of wrongdoing to your credit and you can be sure they haven't been sending any notices to another person.

Credit Monitoring is, by itself, only a partial solution, and not a perfect one at that. An information technology manager discovered this for herself. Six months after she and her husband started having their credit monitored, she discovered that at least 26 credit cards had been applied for, several cars had been financed, and a home mortgage had been taken out using her husband's SSN. They were not notified of any of this by their credit monitoring.[53] Credit monitoring only works so long as creditors report activities to the bureaus, and it may come as a surprise, but thieves somehow steer toward the ones that don't. According to experts in the banking industry, less than half of the merchants and banks actually check your Credit Report before issuing credit![54] And, by the way, monitoring does nothing to restore your identity once it is stolen. It is like having a smoke detector in your house. It lets you know that there is a problem, but it doesn't do anything to put out the fire. As the name implies, credit monitoring helps only with Financial Identity Theft. It can't do anything if someone commits any of the other types of Identity Theft. So while we recommend that you have it, don't expect it to do everything.

Data Monitoring

Data monitoring may eventually replace credit monitoring, but to date this service is not yet developed enough to provide a significant advantage over credit monitoring. The easiest way to think about this option is that when you sign up for this service, they "Google" you (but they have access to more than just the web). In effect, they take a snapshot of everything that they can find about you, including your Credit Report and every other source they can access. This is where The DataBased You can come into play. An entire class of companies exists to compile everything (called Data Aggregators), and so a data examination can find out a lot. This is where the digital biography we talked about at the end of the last section is brought together. Data monitoring checks this information to help you make sure that it is correct. The problem with these services is that other than credit, there is no way to monitor any other type of information continuously over time. It's the

> According to experts in the banking industry, less than half of the merchants and banks actually check your Credit Report before issuing credit!

same reason Europe doesn't have monitoring. Another reason Data Monitoring is not yet mature is that if these monitoring databases were to notify you every time new information came in about you, you would be receiving notifications EVERY DAY, and nobody wants that (not to mention you would soon ignore them). The next area where monitoring may be available is medical records, but that is another conversation and far from being a reality.

Resolution Services

One of the most popular options that gives people the idea that they have protection is resolution services. These services are a great, low cost option -- for the company that offers it. They collect routine payments from you and do very little in return. Resolution services are generally provided in conjunction with credit monitoring, and they give the appearance that they'll solve the problem for you. When you find out that you are the victim of Identity Theft, they'll mail or email you a package of information that will "help" you sort your way through the process of fixing your own identity. As far as we can tell, no one out there has a better package of information than the FTC. Their booklet, *Take Charge: Fighting Back Against Identity Theft*, which was discussed earlier, is freely available at www.ftc.gov/idtheft or by calling 1877-ID-THEFT. Many resolution services simply take the information in that booklet, repackage it with their name on it, and send it to you. After all, why should they spend time and money to research and develop the same product that they can get and use for free?

Many of these services will also have a toll free number available for you to call to get "assistance." As near as we can tell, most of them use a number that resembles 1-800-INDIA. And if you are like us, then you'll do anything to avoid calling them for assistance as the help they normally provide usually leaves us frustrated and still needing to fix our problems. If you are a fan of using call centers, then please disregard our advice, but if it doesn't work out, don't say that we didn't warn you. Most importantly, even if the toll free number does have a qualified person to assist you through the process, you're still the one who has to do all of the work. That means that you're spending all of your time fixing a problem which was not of your own making.

Credit monitoring and resolution services are both very common because of their low development and marketing costs, which allows for a very high profit margin to the people selling the service, especially since neither requires much work by the company offering the service. Instead, they leave most of the work to you.

Reimbursement Policies

Reimbursement policies are becoming a popular "add on" features to insurance policies. This is a great way for your insurance agent to add value to you as a current customer and create the perception that you're being given better protection. And while these policies can help to defray the cost to you from Identity Theft, you should be aware of some of their limitations.

We have not yet seen any reimbursement policy that will cover the debts that thieves rack up using your name. In other words, if a thief buys a house in your name, the reimbursement policy is written so that it may cover the cost of you trying to clear yourself, but it does not cover the home loan itself. You also need to be aware of the definition of Identity Theft that most of these companies use. In many cases, you will find that their terms do not include anything beyond Financial Identity Theft. So don't expect to be reimbursed if you have to clear a DUI charge against you or as you try to avoid losing your health insurance. The second thing is that the insurance company reimburses you for money you spend. This means you have to spend the time and the money first. But perhaps the hardest piece to swallow is that they may not reimburse you for your expenses. If you find out that four months ago someone ran up a $10,000 debt in your name, you will be in trouble. You hire a lawyer to clear you (reimbursement policies generally do cover the cost of attorneys), and he charges $3,000 to discover that since the charges took place more than 60 days ago, you are responsible for the debt (we will explain why this is true in the next chapter). You still have to pay the $3,000 to the lawyer. When you go to have this expense reimbursed, the insurance company tells you that since you are responsible for the debt, they are not responsible for reimbursing you for the cost of the attorney. After all, how many insurance companies are anxious to pay out claims if they don't have to?

Restoration Services

When it comes to outsourcing, restoration services are one of the best options to have. They generally involve using an investigative service experienced in discovering and unraveling fraud and taking corrective actions. While they will need help from you (since they're acting in your name), they go and do most of the work. This usually includes forensic accounting, research, and general investigative techniques. There are, however, two drawbacks to restoration services. The first is that these investigators are normally not lawyers. That means that many of the actions they need to take on your behalf will require an additional expense on your part (we will cover this next). The second drawback is that they can only go to work when they know something is wrong. What this means is that restoration services by themselves, while very useful, are also not a panacea.

You should also beware of the product that you are buying. Many companies will say that they are offering restoration services, but they're actually providing resolution services. Make sure that you check the fine print. One of the ways to know that they're going to do a lot of the work is if they require you to execute a limited power of attorney so they can act on your behalf. If they do, then they are likely a restoration service rather than a resolution service.

If it is a true restoration service, the coverage will cost more, though it is well worth the cost if/when you become a victim. Like life insurance, getting $15,000 of insurance is better than none and cheaper than $250,000 or $500,000, but if you have a loss, you, no doubt, will wish you had gotten more coverage.

Legal Counsel

If you gathered anything from the last chapter, we hope it is that virtually every action that you have to take with regard to restoring your identity is a legal matter. In some cases, you can act as your own counsel. But in cases of DMV, SSN, Medical, and Character ID Theft, you almost certainly cannot operate alone. Although many lawyers would have you believe that they are superheroes in suits, they do have significant limitations. First, how do you find the lawyer that can actually deal with your specific problem? You wouldn't hire a podiatrist to operate on your brain – you find a brain surgeon. Second, very few lawyers are certified to operate in multiple states. That means that if your case covers more than one state (and most do), you'll need more than one lawyer. And finally, as with the other products mentioned, attorneys provide only part of the answer.

These services are available and, like insurance, the better the coverage, the higher the cost. Look at the coverage; there are flat-fee services that provide 24/7 telephone access to attorneys in emergencies and the ability, during business hours, to talk to an attorney, get them to answer questions, review documents and write letters. At a minimum, the service should provide this.

Our Answer

We advise that the best solution to protect your entire identity is a suite of products. The protection of your computer is a great analogy. Our computers face multiple threats. Most of us have a layered protection system, including a firewall, virus protection, and spyware protection. The most sophisticated, layered security system for your computer is no guarantee that you won't get some form of malware. However, you are infinitely better off with all of that protection than without it. Very simply, you cannot eliminate the risk. Risk managers know this, and so should you.

One other analogy involving the computer is that prior to approximately the year 2000, we would have thought it outrageous to pay to protect our computers. Today, we don't even think twice about it; we just make sure they're protected. The same is about to be true for our identities (which, frankly, are much more valuable). In fact, before all else, you should protect your character, health and finances. We might not like having to pay to protect every aspect of our lives, but in our computer-dependent, databased, Facebooked, services bundled, micro-advertised, connected-all-the-time world, it is fast becoming apparent we must do so.

The Web Of The DataBased You ™

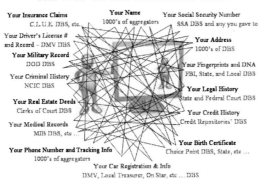

Your Insurance Claims
C.L.U.E. DBS, etc.

Your Name
1000's of aggregators

Your Social Security Number
SSA DBS and any you gave to

Your Driver's License #
and Record – DMV DBS

Your Address
1000's of DBS

Your Military Record
DOD DBS

Your Criminal History
NCIC DBS

Your Fingerprints and DNA
FBI, State, and Local DBS

Your Legal History
State and Federal Court DBS

Your Real Estate Deeds
Clerks of Court DBS

Your Credit History
Credit Repositories' DBS

Your Medical Records
MIB DBS, etc ...

Your Birth Certificate
Choice Point DBS, State, etc ...

Your Phone Number and Tracking Info
1000's of aggregators

Your Car Registration & Info
DMV, Local Treasurer, On Star, etc ... DBS

Just as your computer is now threatened by multiple forms of malware in an ever evolving and continuously more sophisticated manner, the same is true for your identity. We highly advise a combination of products to minimize your risk and notify you as early as possible of an attack on your identity. Just like cancer, the earlier you discover the problem, the better your chances of a complete cure.

Like your computer, you can buy bundled services for your identity. One of the advantages is that the services can work together and cross over. A Driver's License Identity Theft may also become a Criminal Identity Theft, and a Medical Identity Theft can quickly turn into a Financial Identity Theft. A lawyer may need to help you, while working with a restoration service that is checking and correcting, where possible, commercial, DMV, and public databases. Credit Monitoring can potentially discover Financial Identity Theft early and work with an attorney and/or a restoration service to potentially prevent the ensuing Criminal Identity Theft or corruption of your medical records. The monitoring service may be the only way to find out about Medical Identity Theft since there is no monitoring of the medical records themselves. It is only when you do not pay the medical bills (that you didn't know about) and the bills are turned over to collections that the Credit Monitoring will pick up the hit on your credit records. You will need the attorney to help clean up your medical records to the extent that it is possible. When you call to tell the medical facility that the bill is not yours and you want your medical records cleared since your medical files contain someone else's treatment information, you may have a tough time even getting to see the other person's information (filed under your name) because of the HIPAA privacy provisions. At that point, you will need the attorney to work with the medical service provider to get you that access.

You may choose to go to multiple locations and providers to get all of these services. You may also feel that you only need one, two or none of these components. That is strictly up to you. But if you choose not to get any of these, at least you now understand the risks that you face. It is your life, and we have come to the conclusion that the risks are sufficiently high and growing (like those threats to your computer back in 2000). We advise a suite of products, as outlined above, that includes Credit Monitoring, full Restoration, and Access to Counsel. The cost for minimal protection may run from a few cents a day up to about $2 per day for the best layered protection.

Protecting Your Children

While we won't say that having someone steal the identity of your child isn't a problem, the solution to protecting your identity is not the same as protecting theirs (it is actually easier, in most cases). A number of prospective solutions include a focus on your children, and while some of them have something to offer, most can't really provide any protection. Many children's Identity Theft protection solutions revolve around monitoring their credit or filing a fraud alert. The limitations of credit monitoring for adults also apply to children. Filing a Fraud alert has its pitfalls, too. However, since children under the age of 18 lack the legal capacity to enter into a contract without court involvement, getting those issues resolved is much easier. For instance, there is no 60-day time clock running on their problems like there often is with adults. As a result, the best protection you can have for your children is access to legal counsel, because a lawyer will be better able to dispute any problem that may arise. Likewise, should they become victims of some other type of Identity Theft, you're going to need an attorney anyway. If you receive a notice of unpaid taxes because someone is using your child's social security number, it is a lot easier to prove your three-year old is not working. A lawyer can handle this pretty easily, and the same applies to most other areas. Just be aware that if the child's ID is being used in one area, you may need to look to clear it up in others, just like your own. A medical bill for services that they did not receive also probably means medical records need to be expunged to the extent possible. We certainly aren't suggesting that you shouldn't be concerned about your children's identities, but we do believe that their risk is significantly less than yours, and it is generally much easier to correct if it does happen. Last, unfortunately, we often find that children's IDs are often used by relatives. This family connection often makes the cleanup process more complicated, as you can imagine.

A Last Reminder

Whatever you choose to do to protect yourself, take the time to go through due diligence to make sure you are getting what you think is appropriate for the needs of you and your family. Be wary of guarantees and promises. Look at the fine print to see what isn't covered. And remember, nothing can totally prevent Identity Theft from happening, and there is no way to be sure that your identity will ever be fully restored once it's been stolen. For more information about our recommendations on specific products, please see our website www.thedatabasedyou.com.

We're from the Government
and We're Here to Help!

If you're looking for the overall solution to come from the government, we have some bad news for you. The cavalry isn't coming to your rescue. But before you get too excited, it isn't really all their fault. When the government has the choice to invest tax money, they have to decide whether to try to prevent another 9/11, to pay for Social Security, or to try to stop Identity Theft. And while law enforcement personnel are certainly sympathetic, they still have crimes like murder to deal with. Better solutions are being developed, but they take time to test and implement.

Why can't the government move faster? The truth is, you really don't want them to move any faster. Eugene McCarthy said it best when he noted, "An efficient bureaucracy is the greatest threat to liberty."[55] While this is no time for discussion on government, believe us when we say that rarely are we better off in the long run when the government circumvents the process to pass laws quickly. Laws that are rushed to be passed often have large loopholes, usually ones that give the government more power. It also leads to worse unintended consequences, ones that we won't like. The laws that make it through the longer ratification process are usually ones that are the least offensive to anyone because of all of the competing interests, making them less likely to have real teeth. Despite all of that, there are still some things that the government has been able to do, and they are working to do more.

The President's Task Force on Identity Theft has made some significant progress toward moving the country in the right direction. While their primary focus is to fix the problems within the government, they have also made other important recommendations, such as the creation of a standard Identity Theft Police Report.[56] This would be valuable for many reasons. The most important reason is that without such a standardized form, you as a victim will likely have to fill out multiple forms in every jurisdiction where you're affected. This is if you can even get someone to give you enough attention to show you what forms to fill out (not uncommon). If the crime takes place in one state, the criminal is in another state, and you live in a third, who has jurisdiction? While such problems wouldn't be completely solved by adopting a common form, standardization would reduce the administrative problems associated with the issue and would make sure that all of the pertinent information is captured in the reporting process.

In mentioning the fact that many of the actions in the Task Force strategic plan dealt with government operations you may think that they are ignoring you as a citizen. We would never agree with that sentiment. First, the government is the primary focus because it is about the only thing that the Task Force can directly influence. Also, it is only when the government is cleaning its own house that it can reasonably expect the private sector to follow. One area that is particularly emphasized is law enforcement. This is the group of people that can help you most. As law enforcement gets more help, they will be better able to fight the crimes and help you out. The police and prosecutors do not like open files – cold cases notwithstanding. They like to bring cases through prosecution. Since many prosecutors are elected, opening a lot of files that you aren't likely to close for your opposition to beat you over the head with is not encouraged. As a result, you do not get encouraged to file a claim.

Current Laws

Regulation E is probably the most important rule when it comes to credit card and bankcard fraud, as well as Financial Identity Theft. This rule limits your liability from credit card fraud to $50. For bankcard fraud and fraud from electronic transfers, you have more liability. Like credit card fraud, your liability is limited to $50, at least for the first 48 hours. Your liability goes up daily until 60 days, after which you are responsible for all of it. If you don't believe us, here is a quote from the FTC's *Take Charge* guide: "To take advantage of the law's consumer protection, you must... send your letter so that it reaches the creditor within 60 days after the first bill containing the error was mailed to you. If an identity thief changed the address on your account and you didn't receive the bill, your dispute letter still must reach the creditor within 60 days of when the creditor would have mailed the bill." [57] Since most people don't find out that they're victims of Identity Theft for 12-14 months from the occurrence date, you -- not the bank -- wind up owing the money. In other words, Regulation E helps in some ways, but it makes you liable in others.

Zero Liability

A side note about Regulation E in action is with the claims of zero liability on your bank or debit cards. The next time that you see a commercial for one of these, try to read the fine print at the bottom. You may have to TiVo the ad and pause it on your screen, because the words disappear so fast. What you will see in most commercials are three disclaimers:

- Zero liability does not apply if the card was used at an ATM.

- Zero liability does not apply if the card was used with its PIN.

- Zero liability does not apply if the transaction is not processed through the issuing company's check card security system.[58]

If you think about it, this is crazy. One of the primary uses of debit cards is to get money from ATMs. And supposedly one of the most important security features of the card is that you use your PIN. One place where you could use your debit card where neither of these would be the case is at the gas pump. But since using the Visa or MasterCard check card system adds anywhere from .5-2.5% onto each transaction, many retailers don't use it.[59] That means that zero liability doesn't apply in practically any situations.

Back to the laws. In 2005, the Fair and Accurate Credit Transaction Act (FACTA) went into effect, allowing people to get free copies of their Credit Reports. The Act also does some other things, but those things apply more to businesses, not individuals. If you've ever hired anyone and still have their personal information, you may want to read about FACTA in the business section.

A broad stroke: the rule requires you to destroy Personally Identifiable Information and Non-Public Information when getting rid of it. That means totally shredding documents and the Department of Defense (DoD)-level erasing and physical destruction of all digitally stored information. Most people think that the rules only apply to hard drives on computers. As we mentioned before, copiers, fax machines, and printers can store hundreds of thousands of pages. Have you sent anyone's personal information out the door with your old copiers or faxes? You may have sent out doctor's or psychiatrist's notes, marriage or teenage counseling notes, school or personnel records, or financial information. All of this is protected by FACTA.

Changing Medical Records

As we previously mentioned, if you are the victim of Medical Identity Theft, changing or fixing your medical record to remove erroneous information is difficult at best and, in some cases, is impossible. It is only since the advent of the Health Information Portability and Accountability Act (HIPAA) that providers are required to allow you the ability to add amendments to your medical records. The law in this area is still terribly inadequate, but it is better than it used to be.

Your Medical Identity and The DataBased You ™

The two laws that provide the basis for making Identity Theft illegal are the Identity Theft and Aggravated Identity Theft statutes. There isn't much to say about them except that the maximum penalty that can be given out is generally about two years in prison. While it may be consistent with other types of fraud, it hardly seems like enough for the damage that the crimes cause. There are some suggestions that the penalties may be raised, until such time as they are, they don't pose much of a deterrent to criminals.

Identity Theft overall is considered a white collar crime. As a result, if you get caught the likelihood is that you will not get jail time until after multiple convictions. Thieves are likely to have committed 200 Identity Thefts before they are caught.

One of the co-authors practiced criminal law. He says that if you want a crime to explode, let it involve a lot of money (more than that of the drug trade) with little chance of getting caught (steal information in one state, buy something in another state, and live in a third, or third world country). If you really want it to exponentially grow, then make it a crime when there is little chance of jail until multiple convictions. You get the picture: this crime isn't going away. The victims do not consider the crime to be minor. The charts below of actual reported losses and the emotional impact may help.

The place where most of the laws are being passed is at the state level. One of the most common was started by California. In the event that your information is lost or stolen, the party that lost the data must inform you. Since the California law was passed, many states have passed some version of this law. California may have started a trend, but by no means are they the only ones who are concerned. Several other states have aspects of their Identity Theft laws that are important and should be included by other states. Arkansas includes medical records in the information that is covered. North Carolina is one of the few states to include paper records, and it also has a tough treble damages provision. Illinois is the first state to link data breach notification to Identity Theft. Many states, most notably Florida and Ohio, include a time limit by which you have to be notified. One of the trends now beginning to appear involves setting a "harm threshold" — meaning that companies don't have to send out notifications unless a big enough breach has occurred. Despite how that sounds, this is a good thing. There has been no direct link established between data loss and Identity Theft. Because there is no link, it is important to limit the notifications to only those times when you face a real threat. If you were to get notices every time data was lost, they would very quickly get to be like junk mail, losing their value through excess.

The important thing here is to understand why the states are passing these laws. The states are in a better position to pass laws that actually respond to the threat. Passing laws is a faster process at the state level, and there generally is less involvement from the media or lobbying groups (although, sadly, this is changing). Unfortunately, many of the lobbying groups have their own agendas, which are often contrary to what might benefit average citizens. A balance must be reached that protects businesses from an overabundance of government regulation while preserving the rights of innocent victims. The conversation must be engaged.

One example of this is the most recent Identity Theft law that was passed in South Carolina. The authors were asked to provide comments. A clause that was stricken from the proposal's final draft held data owners responsible for ensuring the accuracy of the data that they sell. Numerous groups lobbied hard to have this removed; they want to be able to sell your data without having to be responsible for its accuracy.

In the long run, this is not in their best interest. Think about it: they collect and aggregate information on you and then sell it. You aren't allowed to see, buy or question what they sell. Many of the data collectors buy, sell, share, and trade information about you between and among themselves. And inaccurate information about you gets spread to the point where it is impossible to know the original source or get it corrected. As Identity Theft continues to grow, more and more bad information corrupts the files. Unless some kind of balance is reached regarding the accuracy of the data, the eventual result will be that the information is so corrupted as to not be useful.

The Federal/State relationship actually works well, so long as the Federal government doesn't pass laws that preempt the state laws. To date, they have been pretty good at this.

Fraud Alerts and Credit Freezes

To many people, fraud alerts and credit freezes seem like the Holy Grail, designed to save you from all of the bad people out there. Sorry to burst your bubble, but they aren't foolproof, and they may end up causing you more trouble than they save you.

Fraud Alerts are intended to be used in the event that you have been the victim of Identity Theft (or possibly credit card fraud). The desired effect is that no one can request credit or inquire about your credit without your knowledge and permission. The initial Fraud Alert lasts for one year, and Extended Fraud Alerts can be added. For active military service members, Fraud Alerts may last for up to seven years without being renewed. Fraud Alerts also allow for you to get free Credit Reports annually.

Credit Freezes are similar to Fraud Alerts, but do not require you to be a victim of Fraud or ID Theft before you can use them. Again, they require that credit bureaus get your permission prior to releasing information about you or authorizing new credit as a result of requests for or inquiries about your credit. There is generally no time limit set on credit freezes.

Both fraud alerts and credit freezes are very powerful tools; we think of them as being similar to nuclear weapons. And, like nuclear weapons, they should only be used as a last resort because they can cause havoc and devastation. There are two significant drawbacks to these options: the first is that these alerts and freezes don't stop all credit (despite their names); they only stop the people who go to the credit bureaus before issuing credit. Although every retailer and extender of credit is supposed to do this, many do not (as previously mentioned, less than 50% report in a timely manner). You should ask yourself a question: if you were a thief, would you go to a place where you knew they were going to verify your credit, or would you go somewhere perhaps a bit more careless? An article in the *New York Times* included the story of a woman who had signed up for Credit Monitoring for her and her husband. Six months later, she was turned down for an online account to pay off a car loan as one had already been established. It turned out that there were at least 26 applications for credit on her husband's SSN. They had received no notification of any of these credit applications.[60]

The second drawback to Fraud Alerts and Credit Freezes is kind of like the fallout radiation from nukes. Fraud alerts and credit freezes sound great. You leave one in place until you want to get yourself additional credit, and then suspend it long enough to activate your new account. Unfortunately, it just isn't quite that simple. Sure, you can take off the alert and TRY to get credit, but what if that isn't so easy?

Before you put on the freeze, you had a good credit score. You put it on because you got a notice in the mail saying that your information had been exposed by your insurance company, when backup tapes were lost in transit. After 90 days, the fraud alert ends and you don't renew it. Several months later, you go to get a home equity loan to do some repairs to your home and the responses you get are surprising. The first website you went to turned you down. The second approved you, but at a higher rate than you expected. You try to find out why, but they are somewhat evasive. You end up getting the loan, but never quite figure out what happened.

What happened isn't so mysterious. Banks and financial institutions now use fraud scores in addition to credit ratings. There are companies whose sole purpose is to assess you and to determine the likelihood that you are going to be involved in some sort of fraud, either as a perpetrator or as a victim. The best indicators are past history or the use of a fraud alert or credit freeze. If you have used a fraud alert, then you have been the victim of Identity Theft, are committing Identity Theft, or are likely to be the victim of Identity Theft. That makes it more likely that either you or the victim will come in and claim that the loan was opened by a thief and not pay back the money. Banks run their businesses on a risk basis, and the risk for people with fraud alerts and credit freezes is higher than those without.

A potential game changer is in the making. Banks have had to raise capital requirements and significantly reduce risks as a result of the financial crisis of late and government investments hoping to relieve it. At the same time, the Federal Reserve, FTC, and other Federal regulatory agencies have issued the Red Flags Rule (which will be discussed later) which provides Fraud Alerts and Credit Freezes as potential Red Flags of Identity Theft. This makes sense since this is what they are intended to show.

As part of our investigation, we spoke to numerous bankers on this issue. Most of them feel, justifiably so, that unless there are unusual circumstances, it will not be prudent, in terms of risks, to either open an account or lend money to anyone who has a fraud alert on their file. Effectively, the bank becomes the guarantor of the account if they allow access since they have been put on notice, through the fraud alert, that a thief may try to access the account. It will be interesting to see how this ultimately works out.

Guarantees of Protection

Some companies claim they can guarantee you won't have your identity stolen. They file fraud alerts in your name every 90 days and do a few other things that are provided for by law, such as putting you on the "Do Not Call Registry". As we just outlined, this may not be the best approach for you. And if you look at the fine print in their contracts, you will likely find that they will only cover you from defects in their products, not from other types of Identity Theft. This means that if you become a victim of Identity Theft because their product failed to catch something that it should have, they will cover the cost for you to repair your identity. If it is not something that their product should have caught, for whatever reason, then they are not responsible for paying for correcting your identity. To counter the areas that we mentioned previously, they try to have some answers. At least one company claims that they will be able to get you credit if you need it, but they leave out the part about how this is provided by one of their partners or subsidiaries because you won't really have the option to go anywhere else. Even if you are able to get credit (with or without that company), you may find that it is at a higher cost to you.

The extent to which credit is checked and used may surprise you (even if they don't always check it when you wish that they did). You may think that you will not need credit again. Have you thought about any of these situations?

- Getting a new phone

- Moving (starting utilities or signing a new lease)

- Buying a new car

- Purchasing appliances

- Getting a new job

- Getting insurance of any kind

These examples are only the tip of the iceberg when it comes to checking credit. You would be surprised to learn that the number of times your credit history is reviewed may cause time-consuming hassles or other adverse affects if you have either a Fraud Alert or a Credit Freeze.

We are not saying that you should never use these tools. On the contrary, there are certainly times that they are the only option that you really have. It is like using a nuclear bomb. You may kill off the threat, but at a cost of laying waste to your life in the process. So, think hard about using these tools. Follow the advice of experts (preferably not self-proclaimed ones) and use these tools very carefully and get rid of them as soon as you can.

Next Steps

The government is working to provide protections as fast as it can, but the speed at which they move won't ever be fast enough to keep up with crime as it transforms. They have begun to reduce this by passing laws that are more dynamic that can change with the times. This is a good step, but it can't be the only solution. The fact is, we are going to have to rely more on other methods to help solve the problem.

Connecting the Dots

There really aren't any panaceas when it comes to correcting the problem of Identity Theft. We feel it is important for you to understand this up front because it makes you less likely to either brush off the problem or think you can pay just a few dollars a month to make it go away. Even the best solution will require some effort on your part and it still may not completely resolve the issue.

We've laid out most of the available options (we can't say "all" since new ones pop up regularly) and think that you have enough information to make an educated decision on which path to take. Mind you, the choice of "no action" still counts as a decision. We hope that you also better understand what the consequences of your decision may be.

On the free side, there are an almost unlimited number of suggestions on how to protect yourself, and we have tried to cover many in this section. Start with the government resources; they are generally the best. You can look at the back of the book to help you find some of the best ones.

For those looking to purchase protection, the options are many, but be leery of the promises. Most look better than they are, and none of them are foolproof. Remember the words of Scott McNealy: "The problem is that many of the people in the protection business are making noises that look like they are protecting us, without actually providing any protection."[61] A layered protection system is the best available now, much in the same vein as you provide a suite of products to protect your computer. Let's assume that, consistent with our advice, you have a firewall, virus protection, and spyware. You update all of those components regularly, but even with that there is no guarantee you will not get infected with malware of some form. However, you are better off with the protection than without it -- much better off. The best Identity Theft protection provides monitoring as a potential early warning system; 24/365 access to an attorney and the ability for them to review documents for you, write letters and make telephone calls along with some minimal trial defense; and a true restoration program by a reputable firm with expertise in this arena to go do most of the work required to repair your identity to the extent that it can be. Obviously, the more coverage, the higher the cost, but it is well worth the investment. Again, no system is perfect, but like medical coverage, preexisting conditions can be a tough bar to cross once you have been victimized. Also, like medical problems, Identity Theft is better discovered early and aggressively treated.

If you aren't in the market for a product because you've been offered credit monitoring, by now you understand what that really means. While it is of some value, it doesn't do nearly as much as they would have you believe.

ID Theft and Data Loss for Businesses

The following section is for business owners. By the way, we are defining business owners as including anyone in for profit businesses, not for profit or government organizations, as well as any executives, risk managers, compliance or human resource officers, or anyone else who has a vested interest in the success of the organization. If you are not a business owner, this section may not be for you, but it may tell you what to expect from your employer. This section is primarily focused on what business owners need to know about the risks that they face and what they should do to reduce their liability and to protect their business, their employees and their customers. It also covers what they should do if and when they lose data.

Data Loss and Identity Theft
– The Same but Different

As a business owner, your interests are far different than the average consumer when it comes to Identity Theft and Data Loss. And the more that you read the news or watch the media, the more likely you are to be concerned. From ChoicePoint, to the VA, to TJX, the trend of Data Loss and liability is ominous, and you are probably interested in making sure that you are not next on the hit parade.

It is very important to understand that Data Loss does not necessarily mean Identity Theft. This may seem like a relatively obvious statement to you, but many people think or act as if they are the same (if only so they can use it as the basis for a class action lawsuit). While it is true that data loss can lead to Identity Theft, more often than not, the loss of data has less to do with the data that is being stolen than it does with the media on which the data was being stored.

The first thing to understand is how likely you are to lose data. To date, there have been two excellent studies -- one completed in 2006 by the Ponemon Institute, and a second commissioned in 2007 by McAfee -- that have looked at the problem of data loss in business today. Both studies included companies of many different sizes and from different industries, culminating in findings that, for a business owner, are scarier than any ghost story.

The Ponemon Institute conducted an independent survey entitled *U.S. Survey: Confidential Data as Risk,* which started with the following paragraph that pretty much says it all:

> "A primary reason corporate data security breaches occur is because companies do not know where sensitive or confidential business information resides within the network or enterprise systems. This lack of knowledge coupled with insufficient controls over data stores can pose a serious threat for both businesses and governmental organizations. Moreover, the danger doesn't stop at the network but includes employees' and contractors' laptop computers and other portable storage devices."[62]

The examples of risks from this survey are pretty clear. It means that we've all become so used to handling personal information as part of our jobs that we often forget how important it is to that person. Since we handle it routinely, we eventually lose our sensitivity to it and become careless. It only takes one mistake to cause a data loss.

The McAfee study was completed by Datamonitor "to measure IT perception about data leakage in large enterprises of 250 or more employees as a way of gauging how much of a threat this problem poses to businesses worldwide."[63] Between these two studies, it becomes very clear that there is an elephant standing in the room, and few people have been willing to recognize it for what it is.

There is no question that data is walking out the doors of almost every organization. Some of it is intentional, some not. Generally it isn't malicious, but sometimes it is. The question is, what information is leaving and what can you do about it?

What information is walking out of your doors? There are two major areas for concern: the Personally Identifiable Information of your customers and employees, and the proprietary business information and intellectual property that gives you a competitive edge. In some cases, these may be the same, but often they are not. According to the U.S. Survey, companies are generally more concerned about the business information than the PII.[64] For most of you reading this, that prob-

> Understand this: Identity Theft, Data Protection, and Privacy Issues are here to stay. They're going to be "hot button" issues for a long time. Develop a "Culture of Security" surrounding the information you collect and have access to must become a part of the fabric of every individual and entity.

ably makes sense. After all, the loss of intellectual property is something for which you can see a direct effect to your bottom line. It directly affects you and your profitability. The loss of PII is far more nebulous. Sure, you are interested in keeping your employees happy, or at least productive. The fact that they may not be either happy or productive if their information is lost or compromised is a harder connection to make, so it may not be as believable.

Unfortunately for you, companies are finding out the hard way that the reverse of these conclusions is closer to the truth. If you lose your intellectual property, you are the only one affected. When you lose PII, the number of people who are affected is significantly higher. While there are certainly some probabilities as to whether the affected individuals will actually have adverse effects as individuals, it is becoming very clear that the loss will have very negative effects to your business.

ChoicePoint, one of the largest data aggregators in the world, was responsible for perhaps the first data loss incident to make big headlines. In the fall of 2004, the company sold the personal data of more than 200,000 people to criminals posing as a legitimate business. The FTC subsequently filed suit against ChoicePoint for failure to protect the information it held and failure to properly screen potential subscribers. In January 2006, a judgment of $10 million was levied against ChoicePoint, with another $5 million held to pay for damages associated with Identity Theft resulting from this loss.[65] When combined with the other direct costs of cleaning up the breach, their total exposure was in excess of $30 million.[66]

In April 2006, an employee of the Veterans Affairs Administration (VA) had a laptop and external storage device stolen that included information from the records of more than 28 million service members, veterans, and their dependants. As the loss was being investigated, four class action lawsuits were filed. One of these cases called for damages in the amount of $1,000 for each person whose information was lost. For just one lawsuit, the damages would have been in excess of $28 billion -- and that is before there were even actual damages to anyone in that database. Should that data have been used to commit Identity Theft or other types of fraud, the damages could have skyrocketed. Fortunately, in the case of the VA, the laptop was recovered and the government was able to determine that the data had not been accessed.

Fast forward to December 2006: retail conglomerate TJX discovered and subsequently reported that they had been breached and that financial information had been stolen through a tap on their system. Before they even determined what actually had been taken, at least 18 class action lawsuits were filed against them. The intruders took the details of tens of millions of credit cards and captured the personal information of more than 450,000 people.[67] The settlements against TJX were for more than $65 million. And while the FTC didn't account for any fines, their settlement does involve 20 years of strict supplemental audits and scrutiny.[68]

In May 2007, the Transportation Security Administration (TSA) reported that a hard drive containing the records of more than 100,000 current and former employees had been taken from its headquarters. Even though there was no indication that the hard drive had been stolen for this information or that the information had been fraudulently used, the Federal Labor Union filed a lawsuit on behalf of the affected individuals within a week.

Although the cases to date have mostly been large companies or government agencies, not every lawyer can go after the big companies, and you will find that there are more than enough who are willing to go after you and your company. The fact that Federal Law is making you an easier target will be discussed in another chapter. Also, all of the above cases happened before the plaintiff and defense attorneys had any understanding that the loss of your information may result in damage to anything more than your credit.

So now that you know that the threat to you is serious, the question is, who is taking your data and how is it getting out? Both of the previously mentioned surveys have this area covered extremely well. Unfortunately, what you really want to know is: where is your information safe?

There are a variety of ways that you can lose information. The Ponemon Report focused on hardware. PDAs, laptops, and USB memory sticks were by far the most likely candidates to be stolen or lost (with your data on them).[69] The McAfee Study included these methods, but also showed that 88% of the respondents who said that they took information out of the workplace said that they use email to do it, including 23% who use web-based email as the method.[70] In other words, you are losing information in ways that are almost impossible to prevent.

So, who's taking or losing all of your valuable information? Unfortunately, the scary truth is that it's an inside job. Of the respondents to the McAfee survey, 61% believe that they are losing data through their employees and contractors. One of biggest groups for concern is employees who are resigning or being fired, particularly if they are holding a grudge, and McAfee concluded that "it is a fair assumption that this high-risk group is responsible for a large portion of malicious leaks."[71]

Not all leaks of information are malicious, however. In fact, less than a quarter of the leaks are deliberate. Approximately 45% are unintentional and 32% are planned but not malicious. [72] Leaks are funny things. They may not even seem like leaks. Do you take papers out of the office to work at home? How about a laptop? If you have a computer at home, maybe you email them to yourself. These avenues can all be sources of data loss, and the way that work schedules are becoming more and more flexible isn't helping. Telecommuting and flextime are actually making things worse. Instead of your information being located in one place, it is quickly moving all over the world. Outsourcing is another area that can cause trouble. Do you use consultants? If so, they may not take as good of care of your information as you do. A consultant from Deloitte left a CD containing more than 5,000 McAfee employees' data in the seat pocket of an airplane.[73] How do you prevent that type of loss and still get the kind of productivity that we seek as a culture?

The problem is that information is everywhere. Companies keep everything they collect and figure out later what to do with it. We are living in the Information Age, so we have become relatively oblivious to handling it. We no longer think of it as something special or something that needs to be treated carefully.

The converse of this is that the need for information is growing even faster. With globalization, it is not uncommon for people to have their first conference calls with Europe while still in bed at four in the morning. Working through the day on laptops and Blackberrys, employees finish the day on conference calls with Asia. Making businesses run on this scale doesn't happen without the free flow of information.

There is no question about the fact that the economy relies heavily on the availability of information. The question of whether this information can be appropriately managed and protected is still open for debate.

While this chapter has been focused primarily on data loss, not Identity Theft, for you as a business owner, the difference is negligible. In the next chapter, you will see that you are liable for the loss of data as well as for any actual damages that result from subsequent Identity Theft. You get caught coming and going. And since the workplace is the source of more than half of the instances of Identity Theft, curbing data loss will most certainly help curb Identity Theft.

Your Business as the True Victim of Data Loss

While the government has a responsibility to protect citizens from things such as Identity Theft, they also have to make sure that the damages are not overly arduous for businesses. In some cases, these are competing or conflicting missions, but the government is really trying to see that they aren't. Your concern should also be a question of business interests getting legislation passed without Congress (and perhaps the people pushing the legislation) really understanding the consequences of those actions. The Law of Unintended Consequences also manages to rear its often ugly head as a result of passing legislation.

There are three Federal laws that are of vital interest to you as a business owner. The Fair and Accurate Credit Transaction Act (FACTA) is an extension of the Fair Credit Reporting Act and applies to anyone who has ever hired anyone else -- from a company with thousands of employees to a household with a single maid. It also is the reason for the recently published Red Flags Rule that requires most businesses to implement an Identity Theft Risk Management Program. The Health Information Portability and Accountability Act (HIPAA) contains a Security Rule that applies not only to healthcare companies but to companies that support healthcare companies. And the Gramm, Leach, Bliley Act (GLB) (which includes a Safeguards Rule) is generally believed to apply only to strictly financial companies, but like HIPAA it has been expanded to cover more. Even if you aren't covered by HIPAA or GLB, it is worth knowing what they require, because they are the key to protecting your company and limiting your liability.

Most people recognize FACTA as the law that gives them access to free copies of their Credit Report each year. Another part of the law, however, pins the responsibility for all data loss and any subsequent Identity Theft on you and your organization. And just to reiterate who is covered, it applies to every business and individual who maintains, or otherwise possesses, consumer information for a business purpose (in other words, everyone). What does it do? In the event that employee or customer information is lost under the wrong set of circumstances (we have not been able to determine what the "right" set of circumstances would be), your company may be liable. FACTA allows for Federal and state fines of $2,500 per occurrence and civil liability of $1,000 per occurrence. Thus far, the phrase "per occurrence" has been readily believed to mean "per person." The company also is responsible for actual losses to individuals. With an average amount charged per victim of almost $93,000,[74] this is a threat many companies cannot afford to ignore. As if this is not enough, it's also the first time in history that a law allows for class action lawsuits with no limit on the amount that can be sought. Even though the $28 billion price tag for the VA was never granted, nor was it ever claimed to be a result of FACTA, there is no question that FACTA was a driver. FACTA has not yet been significantly tested in court, but that may be what determines how far this will extend. Litigation generally follows regulation by five to eight years, so we think it is coming. An example: as a result of a loss of data, Certegy Check Services, Inc. agreed to settle for $20,000 per individual for out-of-pocket expenses, for a total of up to $600 million. It is important to note that the loss did not include ANY SSNs or Driver's License Numbers.[75] FACTA should be your main concern when it comes to data loss, but it may not be your only concern.

The HIPAA Security Rule has got the Medical community scared stiff. Published in 2005, its scope was expanded a year later to include any organization or individual who retains or collects health information. The original intent of HIPAA was that it would protect the PII of patients, but it is always amazing how the law of unintended consequences can come into play. As hospitals train their employees, the results don't always match the intentions. When you train an intake specialist on HIPAA, you probably aren't going to teach the nuances of the laws, you are more likely to scare the employee to death so that whatever he does, it won't be illegal. What ends up happening is that he becomes so scared of making a misstep that he stops using his brain. A young Hispanic female walks in and gives her information to this intake specialist. But when the record is retrieved, it reflects the data of an African American male who is 45 years old. Despite the obvious physical differences between these two identities, the specialist doesn't say a word because he has been told that he must maintain the privacy of every patient's information. It seems like this problem should be easy to fix, but the education process to fix it is one that many facilities don't think to make.

Where HIPAA gets really interesting is in the application of the Security Rule, which allows for criminal prosecution for corporate officers in the event that data is lost by a covered entity, along with fines of up to $250,000 per occurrence. The jail time for corporate officers can be up to 10 years. Although this has yet to be applied to any individual, do you want to be the first?

The Gramm, Leach, Bliley Safeguard Rule does similar things for "financial institutions" that HIPAA does for healthcare. Just as with HIPAA, GLB has been liberally interpreted to include any company that could be construed as providing a banking service for another entity. Do you allow companies or individuals to pay after 90 days? You may be considered to be a "financial institution" because what you are doing could be considered lending. Do you think that this is extreme? It may be, but can you think of some lawyers who might be willing to test those boundaries? Like HIPAA, GLB includes jail time for corporate executives of up to 10 years and fines up to

$1,000,000 per incident. The added bonus of GLB includes removal of management and the fact that executives within the organization can be held accountable both civilly and criminally for non-compliance.

GLB and HIPAA are considered to be applicable if another Federal law is violated. Can you think of a law that you have violated if you are suspected of violating either? How about FACTA for a start? In other words, these laws become a one-two punch to businesses, and yours will be down for the count. Fortunately, there are things that you can do to protect your business.

The last area that we need to cover is that of state laws. As important as the last three laws are, the ones that will have a far more profound effect on you and your business are those passed in your own state and the states where you do business. These laws cover the entire spectrum of Data Loss and Identity Theft. You should contact your legal counsel and find out about your state's specific laws in detail. Here, we will speak to some of the ways that these laws affect you as a business and what you can do about it.

State laws cover everything from notification upon loss or breach of data and Pre-Texting to Fraud Alerts and Credit Freezes and everything in between. We have already addressed Fraud Alerts and Credit Freezes. We will next go through Pre-Texting, but by far the area of most concern to you is that of Breach Notifications.

Pre-Texting

Pre-Texting is a crime that has only recently been noticed by the public, though it has been around for quite some time. Pre-texting occurs when a company or an individual uses a false pretense to gain information about you. The two major areas for concern to date have been financial data and phone records. In the last few years, a small hoard of companies have surfaced whose sole purpose has been to mine personal information on individuals for a cost. The FTC has really stepped up their efforts to go after such companies and have been pretty effective. The companies that Pre-text were getting very good, often able to come up with people who matched the appropriate gender, approximate age and correct accent.[76] Think about it; are you from New England or the South, young or old, male or female, or speak with an accent? They can find someone who can speak with that same voice. And when they ask for your information, they say all the right things. And since the person at your bank wants to help, they are willing to do so, not knowing that they are actually hurting you rather than helping. The authors predict that the next area that will be used in this manner will be medical records. This will become even more likely once the country moves toward digital records for everyone.

Almost every state has laws on the books against Pre-Texting. In fact, there is at least one state where this has been linked to Identity Theft. The authors suggest that all states should take this approach. Pre-texting is a practice that puts both individuals and businesses at risk. If your company is found to have given information out to individuals who are pre-texting, you may be hit with the same liability as the one committing the crime.

If you're asking yourself why this is important to you, think about this: do you hire people to do checks on prospective clients or employees? If so, did you know that you are liable for anything that they do while acting on your behalf? If they are acting illegally, they have put you in a position that you may not like. If you occasionally have the unfortunate responsibility of investigating employees, make sure the people investigating don't get you into trouble. In the case of these investigations, you may be safe, but ask your lawyer to be sure.

Notification Laws

Notification Laws are the latest thing in state laws. The real question is: how do they apply to you? First of all, in the context of data loss, they only apply to PII, not just any loss of data. That is an important point -- one that can either help you or hurt you. The toughest piece in many cases is determining if you lost or compromised any PII. Some states also have different things that they cover. Some cover medical information, some cover paper records. This may add to the confusion regarding a data loss. The safest route to follow is that if you even think it is possible that you may have lost any data, assume it is covered by the law and act appropriately.

One key aspect about the notification laws that is in your favor is that in many cases, there are clauses that set a damage threshold for notification. There are different ways that the threshold can be reached; it may be the number of people who are affected, the type of information that was taken, the way in which it was taken, and several other ways. It is better to err on the side of safety than to appear to be hiding the facts. The FTC will find out, and if you look like you've been less than forthcoming, they won't really be on your side. One of the primary reasons for setting a threshold is to help reduce costs to businesses and to make sure that notifications continue to be effective. If you were to receive notices every time something happened, you would be like the radio operator on the Titanic who, after the sixth warning about icebergs, responded, "Shut up, I'm busy."

Summary

As Congress and the state legislatures rush to respond to the threat of Identity Theft and Data Loss, they often pass laws without fully considering the ramifications of their actions. We are not in favor of repealing any of these laws; more than anything, we are proponents of businesses taking responsibility for their actions. Inappropriate and negligent actions by businesses should be punished. On the other hand, the penalties should fit the crimes, and you as a business owner have a right to conduct your chosen business as you see fit. So long as you are making a good faith effort to comply with the laws and acting responsibly, you should be free to continue operations and produce a profit. In the next chapters, we will look at some actions you can take either as preventative maintenance or as after-the-fact remedies to protect your company from data loss.

Red Flags Rule

The last piece of FACTA to be published is far and away the law's most redeeming feature. The Red Flags Rule set forth in November 2007 requires companies to implement Identity Theft Prevention Programs to reduce the potential of fraud. The Rule originally stated that compliance was required by November 1, 2009, but recently an extension was granted, giving organizations until May 1, 2009.

To understand the Rule, you have to make a distinction about Identity Theft which we haven't yet looked at. There are two parts to the issue. The first is getting the data. This is covered by a multitude of laws and covers Data Loss. The second part -- about stopping the actual fraud -- hasn't received much attention until now. If the thieves can't use the information to commit fraud, then it does them no good. This is what the Red Flags Rule is all about: stopping the fraud.

You're probably wondering why you haven't heard about this rule. The answer is simple: unless you're some sort of financial institution, it is likely that your attorney or advisor hasn't heard of it or knows just enough about it to believe it doesn't apply to you. But before you go harassing your legal team, you should understand why they may feel that way.

FACTA required the FTC, the Securities and Exchange Commission (SEC), the Federal Reserve, the Federal Deposit Insurance Corporation (FDIC), and other regulators of financial institutions to develop a "Red Flags Rule" for Financial Institutions and Creditors. When the final rule was published, the definition of "creditor" changed the game and dramatically expanded who is "covered." Now who is "covered" is extremely broad.

Finding the exact definition of "creditor" required many hours of work piecing together language from multiple federal statutes, the Code of Federal Regulations and from the comments published with the final rule. Essentially, "creditor" is being defined as any organization that accepts any kind of deferred payments for any product or service. To increase the scope further, the Red Flags Rule applies to business accounts as well as personal accounts. And since the rule applies to all vendors, suppliers, service providers, and subcontractors of such organizations, there are VERY few organizations that are not covered.

The learning curve has been extreme for many industries as they have become aware of the fact that they are required to comply. The FTC has been working very hard to get the word out regarding the Rule, but the Federal government isn't really in the business of marketing the rules that it writes. Some industries, such as Healthcare, have recently become aware that they are bound by the Rule, and they've been working to spread the word. Some others, though, still haven't figured it out. One reason is that many of these industries don't normally think of the FTC as one of their regulatory bodies, so they don't look to the FTC for governance. Another reason is that the Red Flags Rule is part of a new generation of "accountability based regulation." This means that it is written broadly, telling you what has to be done, not how to do it. The Rule is also written to be inclusive, not exclusive. That means that you are covered unless it specifically excludes you. Most attorneys look for where it says you are covered, not to see if you are excluded. So unless you can find something that says you're excluded, you're probably covered. Organizations such as doctors, lawyers, consultants, or other individuals who provide professional services, along with shops that ship and then bill, never dreamed that they might be covered. Government bodies, non-profits, and schools may also fall under its jurisdiction.

You may think that this is extreme, and you wouldn't be alone. One Chief Privacy Officer said that he "would have to apply the laugh test that [he] learned in Law School to the law." The example he used was one of a boy who collects weekly for delivering papers. He couldn't imagine that such a situation would require implementing the requirements of the Red Flags Rule. He said that any defense that a judge would laugh at (as may happen in the case of the paperboy) probably isn't worth using. And taken to such an extreme, he is probably right. On the other side of the coin is the advice of another Chief Privacy Officer. She said that the Red Flags Rule should be required of everyone as they only require you to do what you should already be doing. The reality is probably somewhere in between, but no one is really sure where the line will be drawn. Chances are, the line will be drawn by the courts once they get involved.

Bottom line, in the writers' opinion, both the government and the public are going to require a "Culture of Security" surrounding PII and NPI because of the potential damages from the misuse of the information. All of us have an interest in making sure that whoever has our information protects it.

Now that you have determined that you are required to take action, what do you need to do, and what does an Identity Theft Prevention Program (hereafter referred to as "the Program") actually look like? While every plan must be tailored to fit the needs of the organization for which it is intended, the major requirements follow below.

Identity Theft Prevention Program

Before you begin, you have to set the stage for the Program. Once you have determined that you are covered by the Red Flags Rule, you must decide where the Rule applies in your business. The Program must protect accounts that you deem to be "covered," including any account (business relationship) where there is a "foreseeable risk to the customer of or to the safety and soundness of the financial institution or creditor from Identity Theft, including financial, compliance, reputation or litigation risks." And this applies to existing or new customers. Which, as far as we can tell, should be most accounts. If you don't believe us, just go back to the ChoicePoint example. They did business with a company they believed was operating in good faith. Instead, the company turned out to be mining information on thousands of people for nefarious reasons. And this had significant consequences for ChoicePoint.

The first component of the Program is to determine which Red Flags to use and how to apply them. A Red Flag is an indicator which will tell you when a potentially fraudulent transaction is about to take place. For instance, if the personal information on a driver's license doesn't match the recorded account information or if the account activity exhibits a marked shift from previous history, then a Red Flag is warranted. In case you think it wouldn't matter to you, what if someone was trying to open an account in your name using your SSN? Wouldn't you want the business to make sure that it was really you? The Rule provides a number of examples of what Red Flags may look like, but they leave it to you to make final determinations. We believe that this aspect is one of the best parts about the rule. While the code provides a list of 26 potential Red Flags, the rule states that these are only to be used as a basis for you to determine the best Red Flags for your organization. After all, you know your industry/field, and you should have some pretty good ideas about where your fraud may originate and what signs to look for to prevent it. You can see the inset for the general categories provided by the rule.

• Alerts, Notifications or Warnings from a Consumer Reporting Agency

- Suspicious Documents

- Suspicious Personal Identifying Information

- Unusual Use of, or Suspicious Activity Related to, the Covered Account

- <u>Notice from Customers, Victims of Identity Theft, Law Enforcement Authorities, or Other Persons Regarding Possible Identity Theft in Connection with Covered Accounts Held by the Financial Institution or Creditor</u>

Having determined which Red Flags you are going to use, you have to know how to look for them. For those of you looking to use technology, this is where it may be of use. For transactions that are done in person, this will likely be a predominantly manual process requiring the training of those employees who conduct the transactions on what to look for. Technology can, in many instances, assist with these transactions, but more often than not, the greater the scrutiny given to the transactions, the longer the process takes. Finding the balance between speed and security is not easy, and you will probably have to adjust as you go. Automated processes can take better advantage of technology but may not be able to detect all of the Red Flags you need.

The real goal of the Red Flags is authentication. Is the person conducting the transaction the person who he claims to be? The goal is to have the level of authentication match the value or the risk of the transaction. In other words, if a transaction is only worth a few dollars, you wouldn't need to do as much (in terms of authentication) as you would if you were providing a home loan. The goal is to make it so it isn't worth the thief's time to commit the fraud.

Once the potential fraud has been detected, the next step is to determine if it actually is fraud and what to do about it. While some of this may be automated, we recommend that there be some human involvement in this aspect of the program. It could be argued that turning over our decision making to technology is part of what created this problem in the first place. This step should also include notification to appropriate parties, at your discretion. How you respond to potential fraud may have an effect on your customers and subsequently on your bottom line.

Credit card companies and banks have been doing this for some time. Have you ever gotten a call asking if you made a purchase? Ever used a different computer to access your bank account and had to go through extra steps? These are examples of increased authentication in unusual circumstances and exactly the kind of thing that the Program should include. You may do some of this already without even thinking about it. Well, now is the time to think about it and write down what you should be doing. It is possible that after you thoroughly review your processes, you may determine that you are doing enough, but if you have to deal with fraud at all, chances are that that is the wrong answer.

The final piece of the program involves periodic reviews to determine if the Red Flags are still appropriate or if the program should be updated as a result of changes to your business environment. Updates could include changing the Red Flags, changing authentication measures, or improvements to any other aspects of the program. The authors of the Rule wanted to make sure that the program you put in place is able to adapt to the times and situations that you face. Again, this is intended to help you implement actions to protect your organization and avoid the need for further regulation.

Administering the Program

Now that you know what the program must include, there are other criteria that must be met before you can head into action. First, bear in mind that this program cannot be merely an extension of an existing Fraud Prevention Program. Many industries already require such programs and merely adapting them to include this process is insufficient. The main reason for this is that Identity Theft is such an important issue that the government feels that just adapting a current program does not send a strong enough message about the severity of the problem and, more importantly, if the current programs were sufficient, there wouldn't have been a need to develop the new rule.

To help ensure that the program has the appropriate level of visibility, it must be developed and administered under the auspices of the Board of Directors. For organizations without such a body, then the task falls to a member of the Senior Management team. This accomplishes two distinct actions: the program should receive enough attention and funding to be able to meet its objective; and the senior members of the organization are placed directly in the liability chain. This now makes it quite difficult for them to claim that they had no knowledge of what was happening. So, if you are a member of the Board of Directors or the Senior Management Team, be advised, you will be on the hook for the liability for not doing this properly.

Training/Education

Most organizations tend to use the words "training" and "education" interchangeably, but we feel that there is a significant difference between the two and that the distinction may determine whether or not the program is effective. When you train someone, you teach them what to do, but when you educate someone, you teach them why. If your employees don't understand why they're doing what you require of them, the effectiveness of your program will eventually be impaired.

If you think this is really an issue of semantics, the following story may change your mind. At a recent FTC workshop, one of the presenters relayed a story about calling to get a copy of his birth certificate. The person at the Bureau of Vital Statistics needed to verify his information for security purposes. She asked him to confirm his name, then read the name, to which he replied that it was correct. She asked to confirm the Social Security Number, then read the SSN. He said yes, it was correct. She proceeded to verify all of his information by reading it to him first and then asking him to verify its accuracy, instead of the other way around! While this story may make you laugh, the problem is real. Almost without fail, if you teach your employees what to do, but neglect to teach them why they are doing it, this type of scenario is likely to happen to you, and all of the security precautions you put in place will become meaningless.

In the Identity Theft arena, many people still believe that this is a victimless crime, that there is "zero liability," and that it's really a joke (with a woman talking with a man's voice, etc.) and who really cares if the bank gets stiffed. As you now know, it matters and education is important.

The Identity Theft Prevention Program can't include every possibility for what might happen, so you should probably figure out how to educate your employees so that they can act appropriately to cover those events not explicitly written into the program. Training is important, as well. People still need to know what to do. Make sure that, where appropriate, training is role specific, not just a generic training on the program. The employees who don't have specific functions regarding the program should get generic training (in addition to the education).

Finally, we suggest that you document the training for each employee. When something happens, you should be able to prove that you not only have the program in place, but that your people have been properly trained. A good example of this occurred in the State of Ohio. In 2007, an intern had a laptop stolen with more than 800,000 records on it. His response in the media was that he had not been properly trained. The state had no way to disprove that claim, which made things very difficult for his management team. We suggest that you not fall into the same trap. This example also shows that no one is exempt from the danger or the requirements. Government organizations, educational institutions, and other entities are often quick to believe that they are exempt, but there are too many instances, such as the one above, where it is clear that they are not. In fact, although you may not be legally responsible, the political fallout from the loss is often worse than the loss itself. Everyone wants a scapegoat. And don't forget Murphy's Law. The person you failed to train and the account you chose not to protect will be exactly where the problem occurs.

Promoting your Protection

If you're doing the right things to protect your customers, shouldn't you maximize the benefits? If you're protecting your customers better than your competitors, let your customers or potential customers know it. More and more, customers are demanding that the people with whom they do business are properly securing their information. If you are doing the right thing for them, then why not use it to your benefit? Turn your efforts into a profit-generating investment. Just as some advocate that they are ISO 9000 compliant, you can advertise that you are Red Flag compliant and that you take the protection of your customers' private information seriously.

Being a Good Steward

While the Red Flags Rule does not cover the protection of your employees, we believe that your team should receive the same level of care and protection that you set for your customers. If you look at the sample Red Flags from the rule, you will see many that could be applied to the hiring process. Applying them consistently to both your customers and your employees shows your team that you care about their protection and that they are valuable to you. Additionally, if someone is presenting fraudulent documents or attempting to come to work for you under false pretenses, wouldn't they be more likely to commit the types of fraud we are trying to prevent? We certainly think so. Just a reminder: more than half of Identity Theft is committed by employees.[77]

Red Flags Rule Wrap Up

Perhaps the best way to look at this is as a new standard of care. Prior to OSHA, no one gave much thought to standards of care for workplace safety. Once in place, people complained but eventually complied. Then along came the American Disabilities Act (ADA), and now we have handicapped parking and bathrooms everywhere. Nobody questioned whether or not they would comply, they just did it. The Red Flags Rule now is doing the same thing for fraud prevention and data protection.

The Red Flags Rule offers the best efforts made by the Federal government to prevent Identity Theft. But make no mistake, they have put the onus for this crime squarely on your shoulders. Taking action to meet the requirements of the Red Flags Rule won't eliminate your liability, but it will certainly help reduce it.

States are passing new laws each year regarding Identity Theft, Privacy, Data Loss, and Data Protection. The protection of our personal information is becoming a part of the business landscape. Very simply, the rules have changed, and therefore we must, as well.

Preparing for the Attack

If the last chapters make it sound as though the government has served you up for lunch when it comes to Data Loss and Identity Theft, you're not far off -- even though some laws, particularly the Red Flags Rule, are meant to help you. That doesn't mean that you have to sit there and wait for it. It also doesn't mean that you can't protect yourself and your business. These laws require actions to be taken to reduce or mitigate the risk, and if you do so, you may find that you are a bit harder to touch.

According to the McAfee study, fully a third of the companies surveyed believe that if they were the victim of a major data loss, they would be forced out of business.[78] They further estimate that the cost to a business from a data loss would be approximately $1.82 million. That includes not only the damage from the information going out, but also the costs involved with informing individuals, setting up call centers to receive complaints and questions, setting up websites to deal with more questions and complaints, upgrading security and providing additional training for employees, and establishing public relations and marketing campaigns to protect or resurrect your company image. And this does not include the cost of lost business. *CIO Magazine* ran an article that talked about ID Theft as "The Coming Pandemic." In it, they stated that "if you experience a security breach, 20% of your afflicted customer base will no longer do business with you, 40% will consider ending the relationship, and 5% will be hiring lawyers."[79] The costs also do not include the legal expenses needed to fight a class action lawsuit or the cash required if a settlement is reached.

But you say, "I'm not in big business." One of the saddest and scariest stories we have heard is that of a Public Accountant in a small community. After a thief came in and stole the hard drives from two computers, he had to send out notifications. He had no idea how much that really cost to do. He had to hire an attorney. He got called by the FTC telling him exactly what he did and should have done, as well as what he needed to do. More importantly, people he had known for years came into his office and cursed him out for losing their information.

When you look at such risk, what are you willing to do to prevent catastrophic damage? You may not be able to avoid all of these costs, but there are a number of ways you can reduce your exposure. Betsy Broder, an official with the FTC, told the *ABA Journal* that "we're not looking for a perfect system... we need to see that you've taken reasonable steps to protect your customers' information."[80]

So, what do reasonable steps, or as we like to say, a good faith effort, look like? This is a great question. The first thing is to take actions that help you to meet the requirements of the HIPAA Security Rule and GLB Safeguard Rule. They require that every company have an information security officer appointed. We suggest that you make sure that it isn't you! Entities are also required to have a policy for the use, handling, and storage of PII. The FTC's Ms. Broder explained that "at the basic level...that means all businesses need to have a plan in writing describing how customer [and employee] data is to be secured and an officer on staff [who's] responsible for implementing that plan."[81] Finally, it is required that you provide training for all employees regarding the policy (we suggest including information about who the Information Security Officer is) and how they are supposed to handle the PII. This should include a list of the consequences they face if there is a failure to comply. Although not required, we highly encourage you to document the fact that this training has been completed. These steps all help to show that you are making a good faith effort to comply with laws. A last word from Ms. Broder, "Most small businesses cannot be expected to hire a full time privacy specialist, but all businesses must be able to show they have a security plan in place."[82] Even if you are not covered by HIPAA or GLB, these steps are powerful allies when it comes to defending yourself from lawsuits. Whether you are protecting data, keeping it private, or preventing its fraudulent use, document your intent to do the right thing. Good intentions are wonderful, but tangible evidence that those intentions have been acted upon works much better in court.

You may also wish to offer protection for your employees against the loss of any data or Identity Theft. Not only does this give your team better confidence in you, it reduces their ability to complain in the event that their data is lost. According to Business and Legal Reports, a good "solution that provides an affirmative defense against potential fines, fees, and lawsuits is to offer some sort of Identity Theft protection as an employee benefit. An employee can choose whether or not to pay for this benefit. The key is to make the protection available, and have a mandatory meeting on Identity Theft."[83] Making sure that you have offered such a benefit is a good indication that you have taken strong steps to ensure that your employees are protected in the event of a data loss (either at your hands or the hands of a third party).

As for your computers, you definitely have a responsibility to protect your network and your data. Most people think that if you can work with IT, then you can do the security for it. That is an unfortunate idea that you must discard immediately. Security is a discipline that requires knowledge and experience. It is NOT just another aspect of IT. As such, we can't tell you exactly what you should do, but we will give you a couple of suggestions. The following five items are areas to examine that were mentioned in a memo published by the Office of Management and Budget (OMB) as guidance for Federal agencies:

- Encryption. Encrypt... all data on mobile computers/devices carrying agency data unless the data is determined not to be sensitive

- Control Remote Access. Allow remote access only with two-factor authentication where one of the factors is provided by a device separate from the computer gaining access

- Time-Out Function. Use a "time-out" function for remote access and mobile devices requiring user re-authentication after thirty minutes of inactivity

- Log and Verify. Log all computer-readable data extracts from databases holding sensitive information and verify each extract, including whether sensitive data has been erased within 90 days or its use is still required

- Ensure Understanding of Responsibilities. Ensure all individuals with authorized access to personally identifiable information and their supervisors sign at least annually a document clearly describing their responsibilities[84]

These are good suggestions, but by no means do they constitute a complete list. You will be best served by getting advice from a computer security specialist.

Since only 6% of the companies in the McAfee study could say for certain that they hadn't lost any data over the past two years, there is a good chance that it will happen to you.[85] You should be prepared. The President's Task Force on Identity Theft refers to this as a Breach Notification Plan, but it covers more than the name implies. Between the OMB memo and the Task Force recommendations (both of which are available online), they have compiled a good list of actions you can take to reduce the risk of data loss and preparations to take for when it does happen.

In order to know when you have lost sensitive data, you need to identify where all of your data is. This, by itself, is a daunting task, but one that is very important. If you don't know what you have, you will never be sure of what's been taken. It also makes good business sense, but you don't need us to tell you that. Try to make sure that the place where you have an inventory of your data is not with the data itself. Also, this inventory should be dynamic -- able to change as the information changes. Assign risk values to the information you have. What data, if taken, can cause BIG problems and what will merely be inconvenient to remedy? If you want to take advantage of technology, there are software products available that can do much of this for you. For some industries, this is a requirement. Once you know what you have and know the risk associated with it, review your current holdings and eliminate anything that you can.[86] You should be ruthless as you pare it down. If you don't absolutely need it, get rid of it. It is far more likely to be a liability than it is to be an asset. By the way, don't just do this once. You should go through this process on a regular basis. This is true whether you are a Fortune 500 company, a small business or a government entity. The FTC spends a full day each year doing this. Everyone, from the Chairman on down, participates.[87] You can also look for alternatives. We have already talked about protecting the information that remains, so there is one task left.

The larger you are, the more complicated your issue. But do not think for a moment that you are exempt if you're a small business. Actually, the smaller you are, the easier this may be to accomplish. Chances are, if you are a small business, you only have a few computers to deal with. However you may have much of the information in printed documents which must be protected, in locked filing cabinets for example. Segregating the PII and NPI becomes a much easier task.

You need to have a plan in place for when the information does disappear. Start by identifying a core management group that will convene the moment a potential loss of personal information has been detected. This group should bring different responsibilities to the table and be able to cover all important areas for you. At the very least, you should include the people responsible for IT, Legal, Privacy, Security, Administration, as well as some members of senior management. You may certainly include others as you feel appropriate, but this is a good start. Prepare scenarios for information leaving your system. Not only will this help you respond to a loss of data, but it also helps reduce your overall liability and risk because you have taken reasonable steps to prepare. The group does not need to meet often, but it should meet periodically to make sure that scenarios are current and response plans are up to date.[88] This is a good idea even if you are a small business or local municipality. In these cases, one person may be filling multiple roles. The FTC Mitigation Plan may serve as a great starting point for you. The key is to plan ahead where you can.

These steps should be taken before you lose the data. Although we will next show you the actions to take following a loss of data, the steps above provide much more protection for you if you enact them first. In other words, get your health insurance before you are diagnosed with an illness. You may wish to purchase insurance against such a loss. You should know that most coverage is carefully written and can be very expensive. Consult with your broker and your attorney. There are a multitude of services that it may cover, and you need to find the right ones for you.

Triage

If you chose not to take any actions about data loss and you are now the victim, there are a number things that you should do.

After determining that there has been a breach, you have to figure out what was compromised (this is where prep work really helps). You will now know exactly what was taken. If you haven't done your homework, make your best guess, erring to the side of caution. Unfortunately, caution and what you would prefer are generally the opposite directions from each other. Once you've figured out what's been taken, complete a risk assessment on the missing information. Does it meet the threshold required for a breach notification? Again, it is important for you to know the laws of the states in which you do business because they will determine whether or not there is a damage threshold and, if so, what it is. There are five factors that play a key role in determining the damage level associated with the breach:

The Nature of the Data Elements Breached

- The Number of Individuals Affected

- The Likelihood that the Information is Accessible and Usable

- The Likelihood that the Breach May Lead to Harm

- The Ability of the Organization to Mitigate the Risk of Harm[89]

Although these are general areas to consider, they can give you a good start. Be sure to think beyond the obvious. This is a great area in which to get outside help. Some companies specialize in helping organizations respond to data breaches, including what the risk is. More often than not, you are likely to think about the data in terms of what you would use it for, not how a thief might use it. This kind of pre-disposition may get you into trouble.

Part of the risk assessment should include notifying law enforcement. In addition to your local law enforcement, there are several agencies that have begun to specialize in the actions to take after losing data, including the U.S. Secret Service. In a recent presentation, one of their agents emphasized that part of their name "secret" is just what it implies. The agency is clearly interested in keeping information flowing to them regarding data loss, so they are very discreet about how they work with organizations that contact them with this problem. They also are very good at providing guidance about when and how to contact the affected individuals.[90] They may postpone the notification if they feel that it will impact their investigation. But you won't know if you don't call them (and without their concurrence, any delay would be unjustified).

The notification should be sent out as soon as possible. It gives your customers and employees comfort that you aren't trying to hide anything. It also allows the affected people the best chance to protect themselves from any potential damage. If you've decided to send out a notification, make sure that it is in plain language and includes:

- A description of what happened

- As much as possible, a description of the types of information compromised

- A description of what you are doing about it

- Contact information for those who wish to ask questions, get additional information or report problems

- Steps that they can take to protect themselves, which may include resources that you are making available[91]

There are many ways to notify everyone who has been affected; use the method that works best for you (email, mail, phone calls, and web posting are good examples). In some cases, if you don't have enough information to directly reach people, public notifications such as newspaper or websites can be sufficient. Again, it is a good faith effort to reach everyone who was affected (and good faith does not mean lazy or cheap).

Before you send out any notification, make sure that you're ready. Once you put everyone on notice, things will start to happen quickly. If you haven't taken some preparatory actions, you will find out very quickly why you should have. These steps may include press statements, setting up a call center equipped with FAQs and scripts, providing materials on your website, arrangements for protective services for the affected people (go back to the chapter on remedies for guidance on this), and finally prepared statements for your investors.[92] If the breach has a chance of putting you out of business, they will want to know about it. A good thing to be able to present to your investors is some idea about what you are going to do to prevent it from happening again.

Just a final exclamation point about data loss: the cost to your company is difficult to set a value on, but here are the direct costs for one well-known example.

ChoicePoint

Legal Fines	$15	million
Cost of contacting customers and credit monitoring	$ 2	million
Direct breach charges, excluding fines	$11.5	million
Total direct cost	$30+	million

Other costs: Market capitalization loss anticipated at $720 million[93]

Another example of direct loss is the previously mentioned Certegy Check Services Inc case. They settled out of court to provide cash monitoring services to every affected person as well as a cash reimbursement of up to $20,000 per individual, bringing the total value of the settlement to about $600 million.[94]

Some of the less quantifiable costs include loss of reputation, loss of customers, and loss of employees. These can lead to a multitude of problems. Taking the actions we've described is a great way to reduce your liability, but any actions you take won't do anywhere near as much as if you had acted before the breach. Also, taking actions prior to a loss and providing rapid notification when it does happen will make you far less likely to attract unwanted attention from law enforcement. It shows you aren't trying to hide the loss from them and are operating in good faith. By the way, they will find out no matter how hard you try to hide it, so you are better off going straight to them, rather than waiting for them to find you. One unfortunate final comment: we expect damages to explode as individuals and lawyers discover that the actual results of Identity Theft are much more significant than they previously believed.

Regardless of what you choose to do with the information that we have provided here, we hope that you have come to realize that you are at risk and that it is in your best interests to take action early. The actions that we have provided are by no means a complete list, but they should give you a good starting point.

Business Ethics is not an Oxymoron

Why would a book about Identity Theft have a chapter on Business Ethics? The answer is quite simple. Running a business ethically is one of the best ways to reduce your risk and protect yourself, your employees, and your customers, and it's a better way to sleep well at night. The more that you try to get around the laws and the rules, circumvent proper procedures, and skimp on infrastructure and security, the more gaps and vulnerabilities you create.

A great example of this came from an accounting firm that shall remain nameless. One of their employees was attending a mixer at the local Chamber of Commerce and eventually noticed that the laptop computer he had brought with him was missing. Being diligent, he called Dell to report the loss, telling them that if someone called in for help on bypassing the password protection, not to give any assistance. Much to his chagrin, the thief had already called trying to get the password. But this isn't the problem.

As soon as the managing partners found out about the theft, they were very concerned. Their concern wasn't that they had their clients' information on the computer. The problem was that they had their clients' customers' information. They weren't supposed to have that information at all, let alone have it floating freely on a laptop. So instead of just having to go to their clients to tell them that the information was gone, the company was faced with having to tell their clients' customers that they had violated their trust.

It used to be you could offer credit monitoring, tell them you were sorry, and, after a year, they would believe all would be well. Today, with the demand for SSNs for employment verification programs, for use in getting medical services, or any number of other reasons, you would be misleading the thousands of victims if you were to tell them that credit monitoring is anything more than a band-aid for a critical, potentially life-threatening wound.

The fact is, there is no such thing as impenetrable security, and if you are doing something sleazy, there is probably someone out there who not only knows about it, but will do what they need to in order to get that secret from you. All it takes is one disgruntled employee to take the information with him on his last day. Worse yet, what happens when someone doesn't feel comfortable with the fact that you are being unethical? What could he or she do and who would they tell -- especially if your lack of ethics made them feel justified in their rogue actions? If that isn't enough, Murphy and his Law are more than happy to come and ruin your day.

You should also consider the amount of information you are keeping. The general trend in business is to keep everything and figure out later if it is something you can use. In times past, this was no big deal. In fact, it turned out to be very valuable in some cases. The information you keep can be sold to make a profit. While there are still a large number of companies that will pay top dollar for that information, you may want to think twice about whether you continue to collect and keep it.

The more information that you have, the more you're responsible for protecting it. There are several different pieces to consider with this.

The first issue is collecting more than you need. There are times that it may give you more business intelligence, but it may come at a cost later. We previously mentioned the idea that when you use a credit card, retailers are not supposed to ask

> The more information that you have, the more you're responsible for protecting it.

for additional information. They certainly shouldn't require that you give your phone number, zip code, or address in order to make a purchase (unless it is being used in the moment to verify the information used for a credit card). Citizens are becoming increasingly sensitive about giving out information, particularly if it is personal. As they learn what you are doing with the data you are collecting, they may choose to take their business elsewhere. For example, if I have a choice between two drug stores, and I know that one will protect my information -- not sell, share or otherwise transfer it except as RE-QUIRED by law -- and its competitor sells my data to make additional profits, I have a pretty easy choice about which store will get my business. And if I ever do go to the other store -- your store -- it may be so that when you lose my information, I can turn around and sue you.

The second piece to information overload is the fact that we are fast approaching the time when forgetting is a conscious effort. At a privacy conference, representatives from Google presented a top ten list of issues for the next decade. One of the first ones mentioned was that forgetting is now a conscious effort. This may sound a bit convoluted, but it is real. We are now faced with the fact that "remembering" has become saving the data to a hard drive. The only way for that to be "forgotten" is for you to erase it. Most people keep everything because they feel like they never know when they might need it. As the information becomes passé, you forget that you have "remembered" it. It just sits there until someone comes along and takes it for himself. In May 2007, the Office of Management and Budget (OMB) put out a memo to the entire Federal government which required that each agency create a policy to know the location of all PII and that obsolete PII be deleted or destroyed as soon as possible. This is a policy that every company should use.

The third piece of this is the accuracy of the information. You collect information about customers, but do you take the time to make sure that the information is correct? The information you keep, you most likely use to make decisions. What if the decisions you make are based on bad information? Even worse, what if you sell the information to someone else and they make a decision based on wrong information. You may find that you are liable for passing on information that you didn't verify as accurate. If you don't collect it, you won't have to make sure that it is correct. On the other hand, if you sell information about someone for a profit and it is inaccurate and they suffer as a result of the actions taken by the person who received the information... you get the picture.

Recently in South Carolina, a number of aggregators of information actively opposed a proposal in the new Identity Theft law requiring them to set up systems allowing individuals to see what information is being sold about them and to make it possible to clean up inaccurate information. Think about that. If they sell incorrect information resulting in damages to you, can they take the position that it's an innocent error and that they shouldn't be held responsible when they won't let you see what it is or have the chance to correct it?

Another piece is taking care of your employees and customers. Companies have really started to skimp on this, and it is beginning to bite them back. If you are taking as much as you can from your employees and customers, worried only about the bottom line, then chances are, you won't have much loyalty from them. If you're taking care of them, making sure that they get your best, then they will be far more likely to stand by you when you lose their information. If you think that you can get around this, think again. Whistleblower statutes have been passed in many states. These allow for the person who brings the matter forward to take up to 15% of the finding in class action lawsuits. Are you willing to bet that you have that much loyalty from your employees?

Although they are less directly linked, Privacy Policies are another issue that will be a differentiator. In order to read most Privacy Policies, you need to have a law degree. Even if you have one, they still are tough to understand. Traditionally, financial institutions have been among the worst offenders in terms of their policy materials. Just look at the credit card offers you get in the mail. Not only is it hard to tell with whom they plan to sell or share your information (usually just about everyone) it is hard to see that you have options to limit their ability to share it. There have been several attempts to encourage companies to write policies with clarity. Citizens are beginning to understand that if you aren't willing to make your Privacy Policy understandable, it probably means that you're trying to do something they wouldn't like.

This again is where the FTC is taking action. Their proposed rule in this area incentivizes financial institutions to use very simple privacy policies. This is a great example of where doing the right thing can have advantages. Many smaller institutions have seen this as a way to better compete. Since they don't share much information, they are proud to let you know it. Again, if I have the chance to shop at a store where it's clear that my information is safe, I'll take it.

The final reason to look hard at business ethics is that they will provide far more guidance than laws and standards. Many of the things that you need to do to protect yourself are not required by laws or regulations. That means that you can't look to them to give you the way forward. Ethical business practices provide a far better set of rules which are consistent and yet dynamic, able to adapt to the times. When you follow ethical principles, you have a far better chance to come through any issue more easily.

The Politics of Data Loss

Our perception of data is actually pretty funny when you think about it. We get extremely nervous giving it to anyone in the government, but we give it away freely to people in private industry. In Europe, it is the exact opposite. They have no problem giving it to the government but are hesitant to give it to any private company. Americans get annoyed by marketers calling during dinner, but rarely do anything to stop the onslaught. Data loss is just as interesting, and potentially just as schizophrenic.

Data loss is becoming so common that we often don't notice when someone else loses it, but when we perceive that the loss may cost us something or that we may be able to benefit from it, the tables turn very quickly. The same is true for Identity Theft. We go from blasé, reasonable people to zealots ready to go after whomever we perceive is to blame for our woes.

Being on the receiving end of this fury is not really a comfortable place. As such, it is best to be avoided whenever possible. What you don't often realize is that if you're not more careful, you as a business owner can be the cause of your own demise.

To date, the laws have slowly been racking up responsibilities for business owners without their knowledge or approval. And the many incidents of data loss have aided in developing their lack of concern. Data losses happen so frequently, without any "apparent" costs, that most business owners have stopped really worrying about it as a problem. The downside to that approach is, when your paradigm changes on this issue, it will change forever, and not to your benefit.

All it will take is one story to change the world forever. It will either be a case of losing the wrong person's information or a heartrending account that turns an organization from a hapless victim into a nefarious villain.

As a business owner or executive, we want to you to remember the story we have already discussed. Unfortunately, it is both true and frightening. The Public Accountant of a small community had the hard drives of his computers stolen. The resulting nightmare cost him not only his business, but resulted in many of his "friends" coming and cursing him out. It became very clear that failure to protect their information was far more important than any friendship. We suggest that you do what you can to avoid being on the receiving end of that particular nightmare.

One of the more well-known companies providing protection, claiming that they can prevent Identity Theft, is currently under suit from someone locked out of her own identity. A thief stole someone's identity and then signed up for the service protecting that very same stolen identity. By locking down the identity, the real person was locked out of her own accounts.[95] While the company providing this "protection" is under suit, the lawsuits still haven't made many ripples. When something like this happens to a member of Congress or other high profile figure, heads will roll and companies like this one will be in serious trouble.

Similarly, when a data loss or case of Identity Theft leads to the death of a child, there will be hell to pay. We don't know about you, but we wouldn't want to be the ones who have to appear on television to explain how, as a result of this mix-up, a small child ended up dying. The story would be covered by the national media in an instant. Politicians would be lining up like a pack of wolves to go after the company that lost the information or acted negligently.

If you're a politician or high profile executive, you may not be exempt, either. Ken Davis, the CEO of Lifelock, discovered that more than 20 individuals had gotten driver's licenses in his name because he made himself a target by showing his Social Security Number.[96] As a result of this (and other reasons), his company faces a number of class action lawsuits. Granted, he went out of his way to make himself a target. Interestingly, he still doesn't consider that as Identity Theft.

But if you think about it, it's surprising that politicians aren't targeted more often. If there is anything that we are learning from elections these days, it is that many people become fervent supporters and there is not much that they wouldn't do to see their candidate win. Why not steal your political enemy's identity? What happens when they rack up some "interesting" charges (while pornography is an easy jump, many people are far more imaginative) on credit cards they obtained in a politician's name? Or maybe they sign him up for some things that may not be terribly consistent with his particular views (someone will ask, and someone else will tell). Better yet, they provide the politician's information when they get pulled over for a DUI. She may be able to prove her innocence eventually, but it may sink her re-election bid. If there's anything that you have picked up from this book, we hope you've seen how very easy it is for the wrong information to be entered into the computers about who and what you are and how there isn't much you can do about it. When someone is determined to play underhanded (and knows what they're doing) you may be in a heap of trouble (politician or not).

In case you think that Identity Theft is the only concern, consider data loss. One of the most well known cases is that of the Veteran's Administration (VA). As of the writing of this book, none of the people associated with, or in the chain of command above, those who lost the data are still employed by the VA. No one has ever come out and said whether these individuals were fired, retired or moved, but the fact still remains: they lost their jobs. If we were suspicious types (and we are), we would suggest that a loss of data is bad for career longevity. But please, feel free to draw your own conclusions.

The last word is that the perception of data loss and Identity Theft will soon eclipse any actual damage and, if you aren't careful, you may easily become the victim. The sad thing is that by following the tips and suggestions that you've already read, you can do much to stave off such disaster and mitigate the risks before they ever show up.

Connecting the Dots

If you think that the explosion of the information problem isn't going to be an important consideration for you in your business or organization, then we think you have your head in the sand. At the very least, you have the information on your employees. If you don't have that, then you may have immigration or tax issues coming your way.

The information itself isn't making the problem any easier for you. Collecting and storing such data is getting cheaper and cheaper. It costs next to nothing to capture every aspect of your transactions which can be used for market research or can be a profit center for you. On the other side, the cost to protect that information continues to rise. Add on top of this the cost (and time) to train (or educate) your employees on handling the information, and it becomes impossible to win. If you don't take the right action, your liability goes through the roof. The forecast can look pretty bleak.

The laws being passed to help the situation are not always helpful, either. The pace of the legislative process can't match the speed of technology (and never will). The Federal government is getting better, particularly with some of the new regulations, but it can't solve the problem alone. Many of the laws enacted still suffer heavily from the Law of Unintended Consequences, where their well-meaning intent has gone severely awry. Again, they are working to try to improve, but the constraints under which they work suggest that our best answers lie elsewhere.

It is important to differentiate laws that affect Privacy and those that affect Identity Theft. They may seem similar, but they are trying to achieve different things. Privacy laws are often meant to limit access to information. Identity Theft laws are intended to reduce fraud. This becomes important because you have to train your employees for both. Not addressing either of these aspects leaves your organization open to risk and likely will expose you to significant liability. Again, correcting this situation does not appear to directly add to the bottom line, but not addressing it can be disastrous.

Put in plain English, many state and Federal laws focus on making sure that your private information, like your medical or financial information, stays private and only authorized people can see it or change it. This sensitive information may include SSNs, Driver's License Numbers, Insurance Numbers, credit card or bank account numbers, Dates of Birth and others.

Identity Theft laws are about preventing thieves from using the information they have obtained about you to commit fraud in your name. In the long run, preventing the fraud against you will limit the damage (or corruption) to your record and the ensuing negative consequences.

Many in the industry express opinions that the best answers are along the route of self-regulation and business ethics. Here are a few examples why:

- The increasing availability of information makes it possible to virtually track individuals. This can include forecasting people's actions. It has been reasonably shown that you can forecast a divorce by certain spending habits. If you have that information, are you liable if you don't alert the person? What if your information is wrong?

- Aggregators have shown opposition to correcting their records. Yet with the increase in Identity Theft, there is more and more inaccurate information being maintained. At some point, do the records become so infected with inaccurate information that they are rendered unreliable? Once that stage has been reached, haven't these organizations killed their own business models?

- The lack of resources to be able to go after the criminals and offenders has led to placing much of that responsibility in the hands of the common individual through their ability to sue. Since many people believe that the best way to get rich quickly is to sue, if you haven't taken any precautions, you become a much easier target? The people coming after you aren't really fickle about who they sue, either. With the high cost of school, the perception of wealth in industry, and the general distrust of public entities, most people will have no compunction about coming after you.

Self-policing organizations such as the Payment Card Industry have their own sets of rules that must be obeyed. But if you don't have something like that, we think that your best option is to do the right thing. By putting a greater emphasis on these basic pieces of your business, we feel that you will see changes to your bottom line in the long run. And while this certainly isn't a bullet-proof guarantee, we believe it is better than the alternative.

LOOKING INTO THE CRYSTAL BALL

Now that you have a better sense of where we are and how we got here, let's consider where we're going. We are certainly not omniscient, but we like to believe we have a few neurotransmitters that connect periodically. As we research the vast amount of information and data points, our challenge is to pull out the facts and tips that actually matter and disregard those that don't. In this section, we summarize by connecting the dots.

Putting It All Together
(Connecting All of the Dots)

We are saddened that we have likely not seen the worst that identity thieves have to offer. Some studies suggest the numbers of Identity Theft cases have not increased. Such studies, however, often fail to take into account the fact that most people don't discover that they *are* victims of Identity Theft for 12 to 14 months. And when you don't know about it, how can you report it? Other studies have predicted an exponential growth in Identity Theft. Which figures are right?

We believe the answer lies somewhere in between. Ironically, you yourself are the major factor for ensuring that Identity Theft is kept at a minimum. The better educated you are about prevention and recovery, the less likely you are to become a victim. And while you may not be able to prevent Identity Theft, you can certainly reduce your risk, minimize potential damage, and shorten the recovery time if you ever do become a victim.

> Identity thieves are limited only by their imaginations.

We are not so bold as to suggest that we know exactly what the next types of Identity Theft may be. (If we knew, we would have told you about them.) We can, however, share that you may soon begin to hear new terminology to suggest new types of Identity Theft. We strongly believe that, for the most part, new terminology will simply be new ways of describing different ways of stealing the old pieces of your identity.

Regardless of what you call it, thieves will continue to find new ways to obtain and use your information. Identity thieves are limited only by their imaginations, and we doubt that they will become less imaginative in the future.

Law enforcement personnel are beginning to get a handle on how to combat Identity Theft crimes. Their ability to catch identity thieves and cause them to feel the same pain they cause others continues to increase. Identity thieves, however, often move as quickly, if not more quickly, than law enforcement officials. And as law enforcement personnel continue to increase their knowledge of Identity Theft and improve their skills to catch thieves, their ability to mitigate and reduce Identity Theft will hopefully increase.

As individuals become more and more aware of the real threat and long-term consequences of Identity Theft, they are striving to thwart potential crooks. After all, who has more at stake, you or the police?

Class action and individual lawsuits will increase, as well. And businesses can and will be held liable. If laws don't change, business as we know it could become radically different. We are optimistic, however, that laws will be changed to reflect reality. In the meantime, blood could run in the streets. Why? Because Identity Theft, data loss and privacy are colliding.

The rise in availability of personal information coupled with the increasing rate of Identity Theft is no doubt leading to potential invasions of privacy. And while we can't "take ourselves off the grid," we can employ ways to fight back—including the increased use of cash!

When people realize that there are companies out there that have created digital biographies on them that include things that even they themselves don't even remember, they won't be very happy. No one looks good when put under such a powerful microscope. What happens when that digital biography, The DataBased You, becomes more important than the real you and that biography is actually wrong?

Wrapping It Up

So what does it all mean? Now that we have shown you what Wonderland looks like and how Alice might have felt, where does that leave you? Well, we hope that you are aware of the potential problems, and still have hope for the future. That may seem to be misplaced in this circumstance, but we suggest that it is definitely not too late.

So far, we have seen that there is more to Identity Theft than just what the commercials tell you. There are five distinct types that have been identified to date, and they are based on your five identities: Driver's License or DMV, Social Security or SSN, Medical, Character or Criminal, and Financial. When you hear people say, as we do, that they wish someone would steal their identity, you will understand why we tend to cringe. If after reading this, you still think that way, then we're sorry, but there is nothing more that we can do for you. No offense, but we can't fix stupid.

When you do become a victim, we hope that you are better prepared to respond. If you have taken our advice, you probably don't have that much to do, but if not, at least you now know the steps to take. If the instructions we provided don't work for you, by all means go to www.ftc.gov and download *Take Charge* for yourself. And if you are trying to take precautions so that you don't have to become a lawyer to fix your identity, remember that you get what you pay for. If you look to bargain basement companies for solutions, their efforts will probably match what you pay them. Most importantly, read ALL of the small print because most likely they are covering only one of the five types.

We highly advise a layered approach with monitoring, true restoration, and 24/7 access to counsel by phone and the ability to review documents, explain them, write letters and make telephone calls. Professionals steal your identity; you really should have access to the same to repair it to the extent possible.

Just as importantly, to reduce your chance of becoming a victim, insist that everyone you do business with protects your personal information. Don't do business with anyone who doesn't make the protection of your information a top priority.

For the business owners, an ounce of prevention is worth far more than a pound of cure. If your risk management assessment says that you should just respond to trouble after the fact, you may want to re-evaluate your advisors. The government and the citizens are making you the scapegoat for the crime, and you may want to do something about it before it happens.

Finally, we think of Identity Theft, Data Loss and Privacy as being similar to buying a new car. As soon as you take home the new vehicle, you start to see it everywhere you go. When you read the paper or watch the news, you will now see articles in ways that you never have before. You will begin to connect the dots and see where things are going.

When you read about medical Identity Theft and a crook being caught and made to pay the bills, you will connect that you need to correct the records as well as the effects the unpaid bills have had on your financial life. You will also figure out that getting insurance or medical treatment may not be the same again. Hopefully, it will also make you think about what you would be doing to correct the situation should it have been you.

Remember, the best defenses against these terrible crimes are relatively simple. And even though there is no way to make yourself invulnerable, there are many things that you can do to reduce your risk, reduce the time until you discover that you have become a victim, reduce the damage the criminal can do before you shut him down, and reduce the time to restore your identity.

ENDNOTES

Identity Theft for Soccer Moms

1   McNeely, S. (2007, March). *Keynote Address*. IAPP Privacy Summit, Washington, D.C.

2   Fleck, C. (2004, February). "Stealing Your Life." *AARP Bulletin, volume 45, 2,* p.3.

3   Yanez, L. (2005, April 29). "52 Arrested in Fake License Scheme." *The Miami Herald,* p.4B.

4   Elijah, R. (2008, May 16). *In Your Corner: Identity Theft.* Retrieved June 6, 2008, from http://www.indianasnews-center.com/news/consumer/19005084.html

5   Sullivan, B.. (2005, January 29). *The Secret List of ID Theft Victims.* Retrieved April 26, 2008, from http://www.msnbc.msn.com/id/6814673/

6   Cauchon, D. (2007, May 25). *Taxpayers on the hook for 59 trillion.* Retrieved April 26, 2008, from http://www.usatoday.com/news/washington/2007-05-28-federal-budget_N.htm?csp=34

7   109th United States Congress. (2006, March 16). *Subcommittee on Social Security Number High Risk Issues.* Retrieved May 24, 2008 from http://waysandmeans.house.gov/hearings.asp?formmode=printfriendly&id=4979

8   Gellman, R. (2008, March, 18) *Access, Amendment, and Accounting of Disclosures: FAQs for Medical ID Theft Victims.* Retrieved May 24th, 2008, from http://www.worldprivacyforum.org/FAQ_medicalrecordprivacy.html#amend

9   Dixon, P. (2006, May). *MEDICAL IDENTITY THEFT: The Information Crime That Can Kill You.* Retrieved April 26th, 2008, from http://www.worldprivacyforum.org/pdf/wpf_medicalidtheft2006.pdf

10   Menn, J. (2006, September, 25). ID Theft Infects Medical Records. *Los Angeles Times*, p.A18.

11   See Dixon, P. (2006, May)

12   See Dixon, P. (2006, May)

13   (2008, October 15) HHS Medical Identity Town Hall. Washington, D.C.

14   Health care in the United States. Retrieved April 26th, 2008, from http://en.wikipedia.org/wiki/Health_care_in_the_United_States

15   O'Harrow, Jr., R. (2006). No Place To Hide. New York: Free Press.

16   See Fleck, C. (2004, February).

17   (2005, October 29). *Nurse Mistakenly Arrested, Charged As Drug-Dealing Stripper.* Retrieved on November 3, 2005 from http://www.newsnet5.com/news/5205860/detail.html..

18   Gallagher D. (2005, August 31) Convicted sex offender uses friend's name as alias. *McKinney Courier Gazette.*

Retrieved on September 3, 2005 from http://www.courier-gazette.com/articles/2005/08/26/news/news01.txt

19 CBC News (2006, March 14) *Global Child Porn Probe Led to False Accusations*. Retrieved April 28, 2006 from http://www.cbc.ca/story/world/national/2006/03/14/landslide-porn060314.html?print

20 Ndu, O. (2005, November) Multi-state Regional. New Jersey.

21 Davis, K. (2005, October). But, Officer, that isn't ME. *Kiplinger's Personal Finance,* pp. 86 - 90.

22 United States Federal Trade Commission. (2005, June). Take Charge: Fighting Back Against Identity Theft, p.21.

23 CBS News. (2005, February 25) *An Identity Theft Nightmare*. Retrieved March 5, 2005 from http://www.cbsnews.com/stories/2005/02/25/eveningnews/consumer/main676597.shtml

24 Sullivan, B. (2004, February 18). *ID theft victims face tough bank fights*. Retrieved April 26th, 2008, from http://www.msnbc.msn.com/id/4264051/

25 Foust, D. (2005, March 28). Forget Those Comfy Old Rules About Identity Theft. *BusinessWeek*, p. 35.

26 16 CFR 603.2(a).

27 See United States Federal Trade Commission. (2005, June). p.19.

28 Multiple. (2007, April 23-24) FTC Authentication Workshop Washington, D.C.

29 Cohen, A. (2004, July). Nowhere to Hide. *PC Magazine*, p. 129

30 Id. p.129

31 Id. p. 130.

Your Identity As A Fixer-Upper Opportunity

32 See Multiple. (2007, April 23-24)

33 See United States Federal Trade Commission. (2005, June). p. 8.

34 California Office of Information Security & Privacy Protection. Retrieved April 26, 2008, from www.privacy. ca.gov/sheets/cis1english.htm

35 See California Office of Information Security & Privacy Protection. Retrieved April 26, 2008.

36 See United States Federal Trade Commission. (2005, June). p. 8.

37 See United States Federal Trade Commission. (2005, June). pp. 5-6.

38 See California Office of Information Security & Privacy Protection. Retrieved April 26, 2008.

39 See United States Federal Trade Commission. (2005, June). pp. 17-18.

40 See California Office of Information Security & Privacy Protection. Retrieved April 26, 2008.

41 Identity Theft Resource Center. (2007, May 2) *Fact Sheet 130 A Correcting Misinformation on Medical Records.* Retrieved October 20, 2008 from http://www.idtheftcenter.

org/artman2/publish/v_fact_sheets/Fact_Sheet_130_A_
Correcting_Misinformation_on_Medical_Records.shtml

42 See Gellman, R. (2008, March, 18)

43 United States Federal Trade Commission. (2007). *Take Charge: Fighting Back Against Identity Theft.* p. 21.

44 United States Federal Trade Commission. (2007). *Take Charge: Fighting Back Against Identity Theft.* p. 21.

45 United States Federal Trade Commission. (2007). *Take Charge: Fighting Back Against Identity Theft.* p. 24.

46 Consulting Demotivator. Retrieved October 20, 2008 from http://www.despair.com..

47 Gartner. (2007, March 6*). Gartner Says Number of Identity Theft Victims Has Increased More Than 50 Percent Since 2003.* Retrieved May 26, 2008, from http://www.gartner.com/it/page.jsp?id=501912 *USA Today.*

48 Fetterman, M. (2005, January 14). Identity Theft, new law about to send shredding on a tear. *USA Today,* Retrieved on October 21, 2008 from http://www.usatoday.com/money/perfi/general/2005-01-14-shredder-cover_x.htm.

49 TechWeb Technology News. (2005, July 26). *One In Four Identity Theft Victims Never Fully Recover.* Retrieved April 26th, 2008, from http://www.techweb.com/wire/security/166402606

50 Collins, J. (2001). *Good to Great.* New York: HarperCollins..

51 Furnell, S.M., Bryanta P., Phippen, A.D. (2007, March 7). *Assessing the security perceptions of personal Internet users.* Retrieved May 26, 2008, from http://www.sciencedirect.com/science?_ob=ArticleURL&_udi=B6V8G-

4N6NJTT-1&_user=10&_rdoc=1&_fmt=&_
orig=search&_sort=d&view=c&_acct=C000050221&_
version=1&_urlVersion=0&_userid=10&md5=f85751bf5
8511011645fce885fac3cd3

52　Naraine, R. (2006, April 4). *Microsoft Says Recovery from
Malware Becoming Impossible.* eWeek.com, Retreived on
October 21, 2008, from http://www.eweek.com/c/a/Secu-
rity/Microsoft-Says-Recovery-from-Malware-Becoming-
Impossible/

53　Dash, Eric. (2006, Dec 12). Protectors, Too, Gather Profits from ID Theft. New York Times, Retrieved October
21, 2008 from http://www.nytimes.com/2006/12/12/
business/12credit.html?_r=1&scp=10&sq=5%20cred-
it%20cards%20opened%20while%20on%20monitor-
ing%20service&st=cse&oref=slogin

54　United States Federal Trade Commission. (2007, December 10-11,). *Security in Numbers: SSNs and Identity Theft*
Washington, D.C.

55　McCarthy, E. (1979, February 12). Retrieved May 26,
2008, from www.quotationspage.com/quotes/Eugene_
McCarthy/

56　Multiple. (2007, April). *Combating Identity Theft: A Strategic Plan.* The President's Identity Theft Task Force, p. 57.

57　United States Federal Trade Commission. (2007). *Take
Charge: Fighting Back Against Identity Theft.* p. 19.

58　Multiple (2008). Visa Security Program. Retrieved November 7, 2008, from http://usa.visa.com/personal/secu-
rity/visa_security_program/zero_liability.html

59　Multiple (2008, May 15).Visa Operating Regulations. pp
454-464.

60 Dash, Eric. (2006, Dec 12). Protectors, Too, Gather Profits from ID Theft. *New York Times*, Retrieved October 21, 2008 from http://www.nytimes.com/2006/12/12/business/12credit.html?_r=1&scp=10&sq=5%20credit%20cards%20opened%20while%20on%20monitoring%20service&st=cse&oref=slogin

61 See McNeely, S. (2007, March).

62 Ponemon Institute. (2006, August 15). U.S. Survey: Confidential Data at Risk, p. 2.

ID Theft and Data Loss for Businesses

63 McAfee. (2007, April). Datagate: The Next Inevitable Corporate Disaster. Retrieved on October 21, 2008, from http://www.mcafee.com/us/enterprise/products/promos/data_loss_protection/default.html.

64 See Ponemon Institute. (2006, August 15), p.2.

65 Vijayan, J. (2006, January 26). *FTC imposes $10M fine against ChoicePoint for data breach,* Retrieved May 26, 2008, from http://www.computerworld.com/securitytopics/security/story/0,10801,108069,00.html

66 Multiple from Booz Allen Hamilton.. (2007.) IAPP Summit. Washington, D.C.

67 Agency Announces Settlement of Separate Actions Against Retailer TJX, and Data Brokers Reed Elsevier and Seisint for Failing to Provide Adequate Security for Consumers' Data. *March 27, 2008) http://www.ftc.gov/opa/2008/03/datasec.shtm

68 TJX, MasterCard Agree on $24 Million Settlement. April 4, 2008 - Linda McGlasson http://www.bankinfosecurity.com/articles.php?art_id=811

69 See Ponemon Institute. (2006, August 15), p.6.

70 See McAfee. (2007, April).

71 See McAfee. (2007, April).

72 See McAfee. (2007, April).

73 See McAfee. (2007, April).

74 See Fetterman, M. (2005, January 14).

75 Maroglies, D. (2008, April 13). Firm to settle suits from employee's theft of records. *The Kansas City Star.*

76 See McNeely, S. (2007, March).

77 See McAfee. (2007, April).

78 See McAfee. (2007, April).

79 Friesdenberg, M. (2006, May 15). The Coming Pandemic. *CIO Magazine*, p. 14.

80 Krause, J. (2006, March). Stolen Lives. *ABA Journal,* p. 36.

81 Id, p.36.

82 Id, p. 36.

83 Business and Legal Reports. (2006, January 19). Retrieved on October 21, 2008, from https://www.braggliv-ingstonco.com/Business.html

84 United Sates Office of Management and Budget. (2007. March 16*), Memorandum Safeguarding Against and Responding to the Breach of Personally Identifiable Information,* p. 7.

85 See McAfee. (2007, April).

86 See United Sates Office of Management and Budget. (2007. March 16). p. 6.

87 See McNeely, S. (2007, March).

88 See Multiple. (2007, April). p. 2.

89 See United Sates Office of Management and Budget. (2007. March 16). pp.14-15.

90 See McNeely, S. (2007, March).

91 See Multiple. (2007, April). p. 9..

92 Sotto, L. (2007, March). IAPP Privacy Summit. Washington, D.C..

93 Gross, G. (2006, January 26). Data Broker Pays Largest Civil Fine in FTC's History. *PCWorld.com*, Retrieved on October 21, 2008, from http://www.pcworld.com/article/124523/choicepoint_to_pay_15_million_for_2005_data_breach.html.

94 See Maroglies, D. (2008, April 13).

95 Clevenger, A. (2008, May 18). *ID theft protection firm sued*. Retrieved May 18, 2008 from http://wvgazette.com/News/200805172662..

96 See Clevenger, A. (2008, May 18).

ABOUT THE AUTHORS

John P. Gardner, Jr., J.D., CITRMS

John P. Gardner, Jr. is an attorney and one of the nations leading experts on Identity Theft. While others were scrambling to tell people to lock their mailboxes and shred their credit card statements, Mr. Gardner was warning consumers of the potential health risks, Social Security and tax issues, financial disasters, and the reality that they could face false imprisonment as a result of someone stealing their identity. He has consulted with various State Governmental entities, including members of the Kentucky Senate, the Michigan House of Representatives, and the South Carolina Senate Finance and House Judiciary Committee Staff on Identity Theft, Privacy and Data Protection legislation. He has helped to implement Identity Theft Protection programs which today protect hundreds of thousands of Americans' Identities and even more recently, he has been educating Major Corporations, Hospitals, Government Agencies and Small Businesses on how to better protect the Identities and Non-public Information of their employees and customers. Mr. Gardner has traveled extensively across North America speaking to groups and providing training to many organizations. As a Keynote Speaker on Identity Theft, Privacy, and Data Protection, he has presented to the National Association of Insurance Women (NAIW), The Independent Physicians Association of America (TIPAA), The Oklahoma Chiefs of Police Association, the Professional Healthcare Institute of America (PHIA), the National Restaurant Association (NRA), and the American Recovery Association (ARA). He has trained at the American Association of Managing General Agents (AAMGA) University, the National Convention of the Public Risk Manager's Association (PRIMA) and been broadcast live over Ford Motor's Dealer Network to all their Ford, Lincoln, Mercury, Mazda and Volvo Dealers. He as well has conducted Continuing Education Programs on Identity Theft, Data Protection, and Privacy Laws for the Arizona Bar Association and Tennessee Municipal Attorneys Association, as well as Insurance and Human Resource Continuing Education Programs.

Mr. Gardner is a coauthor of Chicken Soup for the Entrepreneur's Soul, one of the books in the best selling non-fiction series in history.

Previously, Mr. Gardner served four terms in the South Carolina General Assembly, and has practiced law for over 30 years. He is a member of the International Association of Privacy Professionals, a Certified Identity Theft Risk Management Specialist, and an Expert Member of Alexander Haig's World Business Review Advisory Board.

For more information please visit www.thedatabasedyou.com

You may contact John Gardner through email at jgardner@thedatabasedyou.com

James D. McCartney CIPP/G, CITRMS

James McCartney is an Identity Management and Privacy Consultant in the Security and Identity Management Solutions Group of BearingPoint, Inc. He is an Identity Management, Privacy and Identity Theft Subject Matter Expert specializing in the confluence of Identity Theft and Privacy and the protection and use of Personally Identifiable Information (PII).

His currently clients include the Department of Defense (DoD) and the Veterans Health Administration (VHA). At the DoD, he is helping to roll out the next generation of biometrically-based military ID cards as well as taking a leading role in removing the Social Security Number (SSN) from military ID cards. He was responsible for developing the DoD policy for use of the SSN and is working to help reduce the use of SSNs within the Department and is a member of the Defense Privacy Board. At the VHA, he is also leading efforts to reduce the use of the SSN.

Fighting Identity Theft, he is the DoD representative to the Interagency Best Practices Collaborative, the interagency working group responsible for SSN Reduction. He also works with the Federal Trade Commission, including working with the Identity Protection and Privacy division of the FTC on the implementation of the recently published Red Flags Rule. He was responsible for developing the DoD input to the President's Task Force on Identity Theft Final Report.

Previous clients include the Department of Homeland Security (DHS) where he helped to develop the core requirements for the DHS solution to meet Homeland Security Presidential Directive (HSPD)-12 and the Transportation Security Administration (TSA) where he played an instrumental role in the development of the Transportation Worker Identification Credential Program, including the original topology, data model, functional and business requirements. Also with TSA, he worked on the Strategic Airport Security Rollout, the program to upgrade the personnel security checkpoints at over 460 airports across the United States.

He is a sought-after speaker on Identity Theft and Privacy having spoken to groups such as the International Association for Privacy Professional, the Public Risk Managers Association, Adobe, and JD Power.

Prior to working in this field, he was a Nuclear Engineer and Surface Warfare Officer in the US Navy and is a graduate of the US Air Force Academy with a Bachelors of Science in History. He currently resides in Washington DC.

For more information please visit www.thedatabasedyou.com

You may contact James McCartney through
email at jmccartney@thedatabasedyou.com

Jeffrey M. Omtvedt, CITRMS

Jeffrey M. Omtvedt is a consultant on issues pertaining to information technology, human resource strategies, life events legal plans, and identity theft awareness.

Mr. Omtvedt is a Certified Identity Theft Risk Management Specialist, by the Institute of Fraud Risk Management, and sought after speaker and educator of the subject of identity theft and the DataBased You™. He has appeared on several radio and television programs as an identity theft expert and has presented to the Oakland County Chiefs of Police Association, the National Association of Insurance Woman – Michigan, Ohio, and Indiana, the Northern Indiana Association of Health Agents, the Michigan Red Cross, the American Society of Employers, GMAC Insurance, The University of Michigan Alumni Association, as well as members of several banks and credit unions, non-profit organizations, human resource managers, city municipalities, and average citizens.

Prior to his current work, he spent three years with a private, Chicago-based firm, working in web software programming, e-commerce software architecture, and business-to-business supply chain integration. His company, JMO Consulting, was a lead HR and IT strategist to MichTel, the Pontiac, MI based firm selected to implement Wireless Oakland, the largest wireless initiative of its kind. He was a nominee for The Crain's Detroit "20 in their 20's", an award that highlights "tomorrow's smartest, brightest, and most creative business stars."

Additionally, Mr. Omtvedt is the co-author of a series of Christian personal development books for children and holds a Bachelor of Arts in Political Science, with a focus on American Government and Political Theory, from the University of Michigan – Ann Arbor and currently resides in Detroit, Michigan.

For more information please visit www.thedatabasedyou.com

You may contact Jeffrey Omtvedt through email at jomtvedt@thedatabasedyou.com

FTC REFERENCE DOCUMENTS

The FTC Guide on Identity Theft for consumers. It is available for you to download at:
http://www.ftc.gov/bcp/edu/pubs/consumer/idtheft/idt04.pdf

You can also order copies at www.ftc.gov/idtheft or by calling 1-877-ID-THEFT (1-877-438-4338)

*This notice for FTC materials does not constitute acknowledgement, approval or endorsement of any materials contained in this book.

The FTC Guide on Identity Theft for consumers. It is available for you to download at:
http://www.ftc.gov/bcp/edu/pubs/consumer/idtheft/idt04.pdf

You can also order copies at www.ftc.gov/idtheft or by calling 1-877-ID-THEFT (1-877-438-4338)

*This notice for FTC materials does not constitute acknowledgement, approval or endorsement of any materials contained in this book.

OnGuard Online | YOUR SAFETY NET ™

7 PRACTICES for Safer Computing

1. Protect your personal information. *It's valuable.* To minimize your risk of identity theft, don't share your personal information unless you know how it will be used and protected. Don't reply to or click on links in any email asking for your personal information.

2. Know who you're dealing with. When shopping online, look for a seller's physical address and a working telephone number. Before downloading free software, read the fine print—some downloads come with spyware.

3. Use anti-virus and anti-spyware software, as well as a firewall. Update them all regularly; many update automatically. Look for anti-virus software that removes or quarantines viruses, and for anti-spyware software that can undo changes spyware makes to your system. Make sure your firewall is on and set up properly.

4. Be sure to set up your operating system and Web browser software properly, and update them regularly. Select security settings high enough to reduce your risk of being hacked. Make sure to regularly update your system with the latest patches.

5. Protect your passwords. Keep your passwords in a secure place, and don't share them on the Internet, over email, or on the phone.

6. Back up important files. If you have important files stored on your computer, copy them onto a removable disc, and store it in a safe place.

7. Learn who to contact if something goes wrong online. Visit OnGuardOnline.gov and click on "File a Complaint" to learn how to respond if problems occur when you're online.

To learn more, visit OnGuardOnline.gov

STOP • THINK • CLICK ™

LaVergne, TN USA
29 December 2009
168444LV00006B/61/P

9 781440 117732